MW00332420

NEW
POCKET GUIDE
to
IRISH
GENEALOGY

Brian Mitchell

LIBRARY OF
CONGRESS
SURPLUS
DUPLICATE

CLEARFIELD

First edition, 1991
Second edition, 2002
Third edition, 2008

New edition, 2020
Copyright © 2020
by Brian Mitchell
All Rights Reserved

Published for Clearfield Company by
Genealogical Publishing Company

Baltimore, Maryland
2020

ISBN 9780806359083

Library of Congress

2022   435253

CONTENTS

Insights and Strategies

Illustrations

PREFACE TO NEW POCKET GUIDE

First published in 1991, with revisions in 2002 and 2008, *Pocket Guide to Irish Genealogy* is now out of date and doesn't meet the needs of researchers today, owing to the fact that ready availability and access to most Irish record sources is now online. When I wrote the original guide, access to record sources was through examination of original/microfilm copy of historical sources in record offices.

To remain relevant the guide needed to be revised to direct researchers to the appropriate websites.

My basic premise, however, has remained unchanged since I first started work as a genealogist in 1982: that the examination of seven major records will throw quite detailed light on most peoples' Irish ancestry.

Background
and
Getting Started

GENEALOGY – AN ENJOYABLE HOBBY

"If you understand a man the first time you meet him, there isn't much in him to understand. And you won't understand Robert McCook at the start, for he is an Irishman, and a deep one at that. A big lump of a man – 6 feet 2 inches in his socks – broad, thick-chested, going bald on top. You'd pick him out as a farmer if you met him on board ship or in a café in Paris. He looks the part." This is how the *Dairy Bulletin* of June 1910 described Robert McCook, then the owner of a big herd of Jersey milking cows in Brisbane, Australia, but formerly a farmer's son from Garvagh, County Derry. With this information I began my research into the McCook families of Ireland, Australia, and New Zealand, and what a story it turned out to be.

Two Sunday afternoon chats around the fireside with 87-year-old Robert Graham, who now owns the McCook farm in Garvagh, enabled me to virtually tie up the McCook family tree in Ireland for descendants of McCooks living in New Zealand and Australia. Robert, leaning slightly forward on his walking stick, his eyes bright with recollection, recalled for a total of six hours the McCook family history.

The identification of a McCook gravestone in the graveyard attached to the old First Garvagh Presbyterian Church (now demolished) and a search of the baptism registers of that church and of the 1901 census returns for the Garvagh area allowed me to complete the McCook story. It began around 1860 when Alexander McCook bought a farm at Edenbane, near Garvagh. He married and raised a large family, with the six eldest sons, Archibald, Alexander, Graham, William, James, and John, immigrating to Queensland, Australia. From John were descended the "Fighting McCooks" of New Zealand. John had arrived in Brisbane in January 1866, and from there he turned to farming in Auckland, New Zealand. He had 12 children, including four boys, Peter, John, William, and James, who all served in the New Zealand forces in World War One and were either wounded or gassed, three in France and one at Gallipoli in 1915.

Alexander's youngest son, Robert, the subject of the article in the *Dairy Bulletin*, at first stayed behind to farm the family farm at Edenbane, but on the death of his mother, Jane, in 1881 he sold the family farm and in 1883 followed his six elder brothers to Queensland. There were now no male descendants of Alexander McCook in the Garvagh area, but in the 1890s Archibald, the eldest son, returned and bought a farm at the Grove, Moyletra Toy, an adjoining townland to Edenbane. He married and Archibald's 13 children were baptized at First Garvagh Presbyterian Church. In the early 1900s five of Archibald's sons, Alexander, James, William, John, and Robert emigrated to the gold mines of Kalgoorlie in Western Australia. The youngest son, Hugh, remained and farmed at the Grove. Hugh married Robert Graham's sister, but they had no children. With Hugh's death, on 24 April 1960, the McCook surname died out in the Garvagh area. The McCook farmstead still stands, a solid two-story house, which at one time was home to 13 children. It now lies empty and derelict, only Robert Graham's cattle being in evidence, and adjoining the house is a substantial walled garden with tree stumps inside of a one-time orchard. In its day this was obviously a fertile farm. By contrast the McCooks in New Zealand and Australia are flourishing.

This one example sums up for me what makes genealogy and the study of one's family tree such an absorbing and fascinating pastime. The attraction for me lies in building up a picture – piece by piece – of your ancestry utilizing people's memories and historical records. The detective work in building up a family tree is just as rewarding as the identification of a family line.

The basic aim of this book is to overcome the perception that genealogy is only for the experts. The piecing together of one's family tree is not only enjoyable but relatively straightforward. I have found through many years' involvement in genealogy as a tutor and genealogist [I started work as a genealogist in 1982] that the examination of only seven major records will throw quite detailed light on most peoples' Irish ancestry. The records being:

- Civil Registers of Births, Marriages and Deaths
- Church Registers of Baptisms, Marriages and Burials
- Gravestone Inscriptions
- Wills
- 1901 and 1911 Census Returns
- Mid-19th-century Griffith's Valuation
- Early-19th-century Tithe Books

With these records most people should be able to build up a family tree going back six or seven generations on most family lines. This is a substantial number of ancestors and an equally substantial number of interesting family stories, as by the seventh generation every individual will be directly descended from 64 great-great-great-great grandparents. I intend to show how to initiate a family tree search in Ireland, and how to make the best use of the seven major record sources to fill in family detail.

There are obviously more than seven record sources in Ireland that are genealogically useful, and many of them are briefly described in this book. This doesn't affect my basic premise that for most people the research of seven major records is all that is required to build up a detailed family tree.

The five major record offices in Ireland that are referred to throughout this book are:

- General Register Office
- General Register Office for Northern Ireland
- National Archives of Ireland
- National Library of Ireland
- Public Record Office of Northern Ireland

Contact details for each of these institutions will be found in the Insights and Strategies section at the back of this book together with additional information on the importance/value of placenames, surnames, passenger lists and DNA testing in researching Irish family history. In addition, in this section I have also summarized courses of action for tracing Irish and Scots-Irish ancestors together with case studies to illustrate the process of tracing both an Irish and a Scots-Irish ancestor.

IRISH HISTORY AND GENEALOGY

Between the 4th and 7th centuries AD, Ireland underwent a series of large-scale changes which saw the emergence of new ruling dynasties, as the earlier peoples were pushed into the background, and the penetration of Christianity into the country. The ancient genealogists then got to work to confirm the new status quo and endowed the rising dynasties with ancestors whose names included the first element of their names. The ruling clans boasted descent from the founder of the dynasty as the prestige of a king was derived from a pedigree of kings with origin-legends in pagan times.

By 700 AD the north of the country was dominated by the Connachta, i.e. descendants of Conn, and by their most important branch, the Ui Neill, i.e. descendants of Niall, who were descended according to genealogical lore from "Conn of the Hundred Battles." Whether Con was a god, an idol or a real person is immaterial. What is certain, however, is that his "descendants" pushed eastwards and northwards out of Connacht, capturing Tara and taking sword land as far north as Inishowen, County Donegal. This expansion was assigned by the genealogists to "Niall of the Nine Hostages," King of Tara in the early 400s, and his 14 sons. The by-product of this northward expansion was the pushing out of the existing peoples of the Kingdom of Dal Riada in Ulster across the Irish channel to Argyll, Scotland and the founding of the Kingdom of Scots about 490 AD.

Many of the prominent surnames of Gaelic origin in Counties Derry, Donegal and Tyrone today trace their descent from either Eoghan or Conal Gulban, two of the sons of Niall of the Nine Hostages.

Those tracing descent from Eoghan include: Brolly, Carlin, Devlin, Donnelly, Duddy, Duffy, Farren, Gormley, Hegarty, McCloskey, McLaughlin, Mellon, Mullen, O'Hagan, O'Kane, O'Neill, Quinn and Toner. From Conall Gulban: Doherty, Friel, Gallagher, McCafferty, McDaid, McDevitt and O'Donnell.

By tradition, Eoghan and Conall Gulban conquered northwest Ireland about 425 AD and in the process captured the great hill-top fortification of Grianan of Aileach in Inishowen, County Donegal, which overlooks the city of Derry and the surrounding countryside.

The southern half of Ireland was dominated by the royal families of the Eoganachta, i.e. descendants of Eogan, from their base at Cashel. Eogan, meaning "born of the yew tree," was in all probability the name of a pagan god spirit, although it is possible that Eogan was a real king living around 300 AD. It is historical fact, however, that by the second half of the 6th century the Eoganachta were over-kings of Munster.

GAELIC GENEALOGIES

The end result of this emergence of new dynasties is that the major Irish families have reliable genealogies dating from 550 AD, as historical fact begins to take over from origin-legend. Today the descendants of these Irish dynastic families are the oldest authenticated male-line families surviving in Europe.

The Genealogical Office manuscript collections in Office of the Chief Herald at National Library of Ireland are the most important source for the genealogies of Gaelic families and of those families entitled to bear arms either by hereditary right or by grant. This body of information, which includes funeral entries, registers of arms and registered pedigrees, was gathered primarily to determine heraldic rights to bear arms. It includes, however, records of a great number of persons other than nobility and landed gentry.

On 17th July 1990, Dr Ramon Salvador O'Dogherty of San Fernando, near Cadiz, Spain was inaugurated as the 37th O'Dochartaigh, chief of Inishowen, County Donegal. The inauguration ceremony took place on the original "crowning stone," known today as "St Columb's Stone," inside the walled garden in the grounds of Belmont House School, Racecourse Road, Derry city, using the ancient ceremonial ritual of the clan: the claimant to the title of "The O'Doherty" standing barefoot on the stone, holding a white wand of hazel wood.

By tradition, the crowning stone, blessed by Saint Columba, was carried to Belmont from Grianan of Aileach. By tradition, Grianan is identified as being the great "royal fort" of Aileach, the citadel of the northern Ui Neill from the 5th to the 12th century.

With the Genealogical Office manuscript collections a family chart can be constructed that, on the male line, records the ancestors of Ramon O'Dogherty, "Chief of the Name," back through 46 generations to Niall of the Nine Hostages, 5th-century High King of Ireland.

Ramon O'Dogherty is descended from Sean, brother of Sir Cahir O'Doherty (d. 1608), who fled from Inishowen to County Cavan and whose descendants settled in Spain, as nobility, in the 18th century. The founder of the Spanish branch of the O'Dohertys was John who, on the death of his father Eoghan in 1784, came out with his brothers Henry and Clinton Dillon to pursue a career in the Spanish Navy, the most exclusive branch of the Spanish armed forces. Entry required them to show their genealogy, proving noble origin. In 1790 the King of Arms in Dublin Castle confirmed the three brothers as being "descended in a direct line from Shane or Sir John O'Dogherty, Chief of Innish-Owen."

The Chief Herald is responsible for the granting and confirming of arms to individuals and corporate bodies. All arms granted are recorded in the Register of Arms, maintained since the foundation of the Office in 1552. The Register of Arms and other Genealogical Office collections, such as indexes to registered and unregistered pedigrees, can be accessed in the Manuscripts Reading Room in the National Library of Ireland. Further details about this office and its manuscript collections are at **www.nli.ie/en/intro/heraldry-introduction.aspx**.

"There is no such thing as a 'family crest' or a 'family coat of arms.'" A coat of arms belongs to an individual and not to a family. In Ireland, however, it is generally accepted that arms granted to the chief of a clan or sept also belong to members of that clan (which usually means those bearing the surname of the chief).

By the second half of the 6th century, the outlines of later political geography were becoming visible. The *tuath*, or kingdom, was the basic political unit. There were 90 such kingdoms in Ireland. As kingship was in the possession of an extended kin-group, known as the *derbfine*, in which all those males with a great-grandfather in common were eligible for kingship, each and every branch of the family tree of the dynastic kingship group had to be accounted for. In Gaelic society the poets or *Filidh* were the custodians of the history and genealogy of the clans. This body of genealogical material is scattered throughout early literature and is preserved in a series of manuscripts, written from the 12th century in a mixture of Latin and Gaelic. In these pedigrees will be found the names of thousands of people, many of whom will not be recorded in any other historical source.

To the 11th century the different families of the clan were held together by the tradition of common descent from an ancestor who had lived many centuries ago. From the 11th century each family began to adopt its own distinctive family name, generally derived from an ancestor who lived in or about the 10th century. The old political unit, the *tuath*, now became subdivided into family clans or septs. The term *sept* means a group of persons who or whose immediate ancestors bore a common name and inhabited the same locality.

Irish surnames were formed by prefixing either "Mac" to the father's name, meaning "son of," or "O" to that of a grandfather or earlier ancestor, meaning "descendant of." The O'Neills of Ulster took their name from Nial Glundubh, High King of Ireland who was killed in 919 besieging the Danes in Dublin. Brian Boru, High King of Ireland killed by the Danes at Clontarf in 1014, was the ancestor of the O'Briens of Munster, while the O'Connors of Connacht were descended from Chonchobar, King of Connacht, who died in 971. Irish surnames, therefore, can be equated with their own unique history and geography.

In the 12th century a new set of surnames, belonging to the families of Norman invaders, was introduced to Ireland. The Normans were eventually assimilated and their names such as Burke, Costello, Cusack, Dalton, Dillon, Fitzgerald, Nugent, Power, Roche and Walsh became regarded as Irish as the great Gaelic names of O'Neill, O'Connor and O'Brien.

THE 17TH-CENTURY PLANTATION OF ULSTER

A new dimension to the Irish landscape, and of extreme genealogical significance, was added in the 17th century when substantial numbers of English and Scottish families settled in the northern part of Ireland during the so-called Plantation of Ulster. The Province of Ulster consists of the counties of Antrim, Armagh, Down, Fermanagh, Londonderry and Tyrone in Northern Ireland and the counties of Cavan, Donegal and Monaghan in the Republic of Ireland.

The defeat of the old Gaelic order in the Nine Years War, 1594-1603 and the escape of the most prominent Gaelic Lords of Ulster in 'the Flight of the Earls' in 1607 from Lough Swilly, County Donegal offered an opportunity for the re-settlement of large parts of Ulster on an entirely new basis.

Movement of Scottish settlers in a private enterprise colonization of counties Antrim and Down began in earnest from 1605 when Sir Hugh Montgomery and Sir James Hamilton acquired title to large estates in north Down and Sir Randall MacDonnell, 1st Earl of Antrim, to large tracts of land in north Antrim.

Land in the six counties of Armagh, Cavan, Coleraine (renamed Londonderry), Donegal, Fermanagh and Tyrone had been forfeited and, in 1609, the Earl of Salisbury suggested to James I a deliberate plantation of English and Scottish colonists. Unlike the plantation of the Americas that was going on at this time, where colonization was to further the economic interest of the mother country, that in Ulster was primarily strategic. It was felt that the only way to prevent another rebellion in Ulster was to create a plantation strong enough to resist the native Irish. The size of the estate, the number of tenants, and the type of settlement, as well as religion, education and defense, were all provided for in the plan.

The first wave of settlers came to Ulster as lessees of the numerous proprietors who were granted estates by James I in the period 1605 to 1625. The second wave came after 1652 with Cromwell's crushing of the Irish rebellion, when 11 million acres of land were confiscated.

This Cromwellian settlement led to a flood of new English settlers. By 1672 Sir William Petty estimated that the population of Ireland consisted of 800,000 Irish, 200,000 English and 100,000 Scots. The third and final wave of immigrants came after the Glorious Revolution. In the ten or fifteen years after 1690 it is estimated that 50,000 people came to Ulster from Scotland. By 1703, 85% of all the land in Ireland had been confiscated from Catholic ownership and transferred to Protestant possession.

By the end of the 17th century a self-sustaining settlement of English and Scottish colonists had established itself in Ulster. One estimate of British population of Ulster is 40,000 by 1640 (with 60% of Scottish origin), 120,000 by 1670 and 270,000 by 1712. It is also estimated that by 1715, when Scottish migration to Ulster had virtually stopped, the Presbyterian population of Ulster, i.e. of essentially Scottish origin, stood at 200,000.

Hence surnames such as Anderson, Arbuckle, Armstrong, Barr, Beattie, Bell, Buchanan, Burns, Campbell, Carruthers, Colhoun, Craig, Cunningham, Dunlop, Elliott, Ferguson, Finlay, Fleming, Frazer, Gillespie, Graham, Grant, Hamilton, Hanna, Haslett, Henderson, Holmes, Houston, Irvine, Irwin, Johnston, Kennedy, Kilgore, Lindsay, McAllister, McCartney, McClean, McClelland, McClintock, McCorkell, McCormick, McDonald, Miller, Mitchell, Montgomery, Moore, Olphert, Orr, Parkhill, Patterson, Patton, Rankin, Robb, Rosborough, Ross, Scott, Starrett, Stewart, Thompson, Wallace, Wilson and Young have been established in northern Ireland for well over three centuries.

Unlike the Norman settlement there was little assimilation between the new settlers and the old inhabitants. The most striking feature of the English and Scottish surnames introduced into Ireland and especially Ulster was their great number and variety. In 1856, of the 50 most common surnames in England, 27 were derived from Christian names, 13 from occupations, 7 from localities, 2 from personal characteristics, namely Brown and White, and one other, namely King. Welsh names were often formed from the Christian name of the father in the genitive case, thus John's son became Jones and Evan's son became Evans.

Plantation names can give clues to the origins of people holding that surname. For example, I traced the Sintons of Rockmacreeny in Kilmore Parish, County Armagh back to Crewcat in the same parish and from there to Scotland. In a will dated 20 December 1735, Jacob Sinton of Crewcat received William Mackie's farm at Rockmacreeny. Jacob had married William's daughter Sarah in Ballyhagan Quaker meeting house on 6 August 1730. This Jacob Sinton, according to tradition, was the son of Joseph Sinton who was born about 1680, the first-born son of Judge Isaac Swinton who was supposed to have come from Scotland to Moyallon, County Down around 1690.

Swinton is one of the earliest known surnames in Scotland, dating from the 11th century, their name being derived from the land that they are said to have received in reward of their prowess in destroying herds of wild boars, which then infested North Berwickshire. It is, however, more probable that the Sintons originated from Selkirkshire, also in the Borders of Scotland. I went to the town of Selkirk, and just to the south of it I found the placenames of Synton, North Synton, Synton Mossend, Synton Mains and Synton Parkhead. And there lies the clue to the origin of Sintons in Ulster. They took their name from the ancient barony of Synton, now in the parish of Ashkirk. Around the turn of the 13th century the Sheriffdom of Selkirk was given to one Andrew de Synton. This doesn't mean all Sintons of Scottish origin are descended from Andrew Synton, as tenants often took the name of their landlord. A search of the pre-1720 entries in the baptism registers of the area came up with five Sinton baptisms in Roberton Parish, three in Selkirk and one in Ettrick.

Prior to the union of the crowns of England and Scotland, the Scottish Border was divided into three districts; the east, west and middle marches. Each march was presided over by a warden who settled disputes with the warden of the appropriate march in England, as Border warfare was rife at this time with frequent cattle raids. The Scotts of Buccleuch, one of the most powerful Border clans, were wardens of the Middle march, which included the Sheriffdom of Selkirk. By 1532, when the then warden, Sir Walter Scott, led an army of 3,000 strong into England, it was the Scott family who owned the lands of Synton, not the Sintons. When the Sintons came to Ulster towards the end of the 17th century, they came as tenant farmers rather than landlords.

By 1700 the pattern, distribution and frequency of the surnames of Ireland we know today were largely established.

THE PARTITION OF IRELAND

The Irish War of Independence (Anglo-Irish War) was a guerrilla campaign mounted by the Irish Republican Army against the British government and its forces in Ireland. It began on 21 January 1919, following the Irish Republic's declaration of independence. Both sides agreed to a truce on 11 July 1921, though violence continued between Republicans and Loyalists in Northern Ireland until June 1922.

The post-ceasefire talks led to the Anglo-Irish Treaty, signed in London on 6 December 1921, which ended British rule in most of Ireland and established the Irish Free State. However, six northern counties – Antrim, Armagh, Down, Fermanagh, Londonderry (also referred to as Derry) and Tyrone – would remain within the United Kingdom as Northern Ireland; it was created as a distinct division of the United Kingdom under the Government of Ireland Act 1920. This Act was the legislative instrument that partitioned Ireland, though its provisions envisaged and attempted to provide for the eventual reunification of the island.

The Irish Civil War, 28 June 1922 to 24 May 1923, was a conflict that accompanied the establishment of the Irish Free State. The conflict was waged between two opposing groups of Irish nationalists: the forces of the Provisional Government that established the Free State, who supported the Anglo-Irish Treaty, and the Republican opposition, for whom the Treaty represented a betrayal of the Irish Republic. The war was won by the Free State forces.

The Civil War, of course, was to have serious repercussions for family historians. In April 1922 the anti-treaty IRA (Irish Republican Army) seized the Four Courts in Dublin, home to the Public Record Office of Ireland. Michael Collins ordered the pro-treaty Free State army to attack the Four Courts and drive the IRA out of Dublin. The shelling of the Four Courts on 28 June 1922, aided by two 18-pound guns lent by the British army, resulted in a fire and the destruction of many important historical documents, including many Church of Ireland registers, wills and early-19th-century census returns.

A major aim of this book, however, is to dispel the widely held notion that most records of genealogical interest in Ireland were destroyed; they weren't.

EMIGRATION AND THE IRISH DIASPORA

Three centuries of emigration from Ireland has resulted in a significant Irish Diaspora, numbering 70 million people. Many descendants of these immigrants are keen to explore their Irish roots.

From the early 18th century, a new feature was remarked on that was to have a very significant effect on the population makeup of the English-speaking countries of the world, namely emigration. At a conservative estimate 120,000 Presbyterians left the north of Ireland for the American colonies between 1718 and 1774. On the eve of the American Revolution over 30% of Pennsylvania's 350,000 inhabitants were of North Irish origins. A combination of bad harvests, exorbitant rents and the feelings of second-class citizenship in a country that they had defended on no less than three occasions in the 17th century drove many of them to a new life in North America.

Many Ulster immigrants in this period came out as indentured servants. In return for payment of their passage the emigrant signed an indenture agreeing to serve the owner of the ship for an agreed period. On arrival, advertisements for their sale were placed in the local newspapers. In the 1770s indentured servants were being sold on board vessels in Philadelphia for 15 pounds for a term that varied from two to four years. The price of a horse was then 25 to 40 pounds!

By the 1830s emigration rather than land subdivision was seen as the answer to population growth. The population of Ireland could not be supported, owing to decline in the domestic linen industry and to increasing efforts by the landlords to improve their estates by enlarging farm sizes. The Famine opened the floodgates, resulting in unparalleled emigration. Between 1846 and 1851 it is estimated one million Irish immigrated to the United States. Only 20% of this total left directly from Ireland; the port of Liverpool carried 75% of all Irish emigrants. New York received well over 60% of all Irish immigrants in these years.

Heavy emigration continued throughout the 19th century with the population of Ireland falling from 8,175,124 in 1841 to 4,458,775 in 1901. Today the population of the island of Ireland stands at 6.7 million.

The United States remained by far the most popular destination, but significant numbers of Irish also went to Canada, Australia, New Zealand and Great Britain. In the decade 1880 to 1889, 804,910 people emigrated from Ireland, of which 635,459 or 79% went to the U.S.A. Of the remainder, 48,084 or 6% went to England and Wales, 31,779 or 3.9% to Scotland, 41,321 or 5.1% to Canada, 39,168 or 4.9% to Australia and 5,950 or 0.7% to New Zealand.

In addition to free emigration, forced transportation of 30,000 men and 9,000 women from Ireland between 1791 and 1868 made a significant contribution to the Irish population in Australia. Transportation was the Georgian answer to the paranoia of the British ruling class to what they saw as the emergence of a "criminal class." Between 1614 and 1775, some 50,000 English convicts were deported to America. When the American colonies were removed as an outlet, Australia was selected as the new destination for Britain's and Ireland's criminals. For the first 50 years of its existence as a European settlement, Australia depended on convict labor, usually assigned to free settlers, to sustain economic growth. To a large extent the convicts were the pioneer settlers of Australia. They opened it up for the free, and often government-assisted, emigrants who started coming in substantial numbers from 1830, and in droves with the gold discoveries of 1851 in New South Wales and Victoria.

The end result is that there are now very substantial numbers of people of Irish origin in the U.S.A., Canada, Australia, New Zealand and Great Britain. In the U.S. federal census of 1980, 43 million Americans, approximately 20% of her population, claimed Irish ancestry. In the first half of the 19th century half-a-million Irish emigrants sailed for Canada, although approximately one-half of them made their way to the U.S.A. from there. Today 5 million Canadians, 5 million Australians and 450,000 New Zealanders are of Irish origin. By 1841 there were half-a-million Irish living in England, while between 1800 and 1850, 200,000 Irish migrated to Scotland. At a conservative estimate there are today over 10 million people with Irish origins in Great Britain.

This broad sweep of Irish history hopefully goes some way towards explaining why Irish ancestry is proclaimed with such great pride, not only within Ireland, but also in Great Britain, North America, Australia and New Zealand.

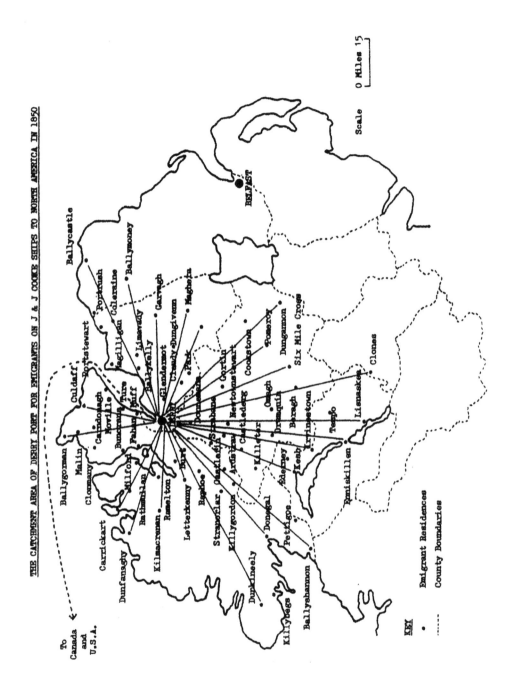

THE CATCHMENT AREA OF DERRY PORT FOR EMIGRANTS ON J & J COOKE SHIPS TO NORTH AMERICA IN 1850

To
Canada
and
U.S.A.

Ballygorman
Malin
Clonmany
Carndonagh
Carrickart
Dunfanaghy
Culdaff
Movllle
Greencastle
Buncrana
Quigley's Point
Fahan

Ballycastle
Portrush
Coleraine
Articlave
Macosquin
Garvagh
Limavady
Maghera
Dungiven

Milford
Rathmullan
Kilmacrenan
Ramelton
Letterkenny
Manorcunningham
Raphoe

Newbuildings
Plendernot
Buncrana
Donemana
Strabane
Sion Mills
Castlederg
Newtownstewart
Gortin
Park

Clady
Pomeroy
Cookstown
Dungannon
Six Mile Cross

Stranorlar
Castlefinn
Ardara
Killygordon
Donegal
Ballintra
Edergay
Pettigoe
Keadh
Trillick
Irvinestown
Tempo
Omagh
Baragh
Dromquin

Dunkineely
Killybegs
Ballyshannon

Clones

Lisnaskea
Enniskillen

Scale   0 Miles 15

KEY

•   Emigrant Residences
----   County Boundaries

BELFAST

GETTING STARTED OVERSEAS

This chapter is intended for those people of Irish descent whose immediate ancestors have lived in those countries with large Irish communities, namely the United States of America, Canada, Australia, New Zealand and Great Britain. Many people in these countries make the mistake of believing that tracing their Irish roots begins in Ireland. It does not; it begins in their home country. It is only by building up a picture of your ancestors there that you will find the necessary clues to make a worthwhile search in Ireland.

In tracing your Irish roots the most important piece of information to treasure, to be gleaned from either family folklore or record sources, is any information as to a place of origin of your ancestors.

Knowing that your ancestors came from Ireland is just not enough. Ideally you want to find out where in Ireland they came from, preferably a townland or parish address, parents' names, the year they emigrated, the port they arrived at, their age on emigration, if they were married when they came out, and if so, the name of their spouse and names and ages of any children. In some cases, family tradition may be able to provide some answers to these questions, but in most cases various record sources will have to be searched for this information. It is, therefore, the intention of this section to give heart to those who think this is a daunting task by giving examples drawn from a variety of record sources in the various countries. It will show how clues can be built up on the origins of an Irish ancestor. Always remember when you are examining any record source, whether it be in a record office or on a subscription family history website such as **www.ancestry.com**, **www.findmypast.com** or **www.myheritage.com**, that your purpose is essentially to extract information against the following three key words: NAME, LOCATION and DATE.

AUSTRALIA

Australia has, without a doubt, a superb collection of records for the genealogically minded. The three prime sources – convict records, assisted immigration lists, and birth, marriage and death certificates – provide a wealth of relevant detail for those tracking down their Irish ancestors.

Convict indents, in which the convicts were listed by ship on their arrival in Sydney, date from 1788, i.e. from the earliest beginnings of the colony. The early indents give the name, date and place of conviction for every convict, while those from the 1820s also provide their native place and age. This detail on individual convicts can also be followed up in Ireland. For example, the report of the trial of Wilson Cornwall, who was sentenced to 15 years transportation at the Crown Court in Derry on Saturday, 23 March 1839, was recorded in the *Londonderry Sentinel* newspaper of 30 March 1839. Seemingly, Wilson Cornwall and an accomplice, Moses Hutchinson, robbed Alexander Mitchell, a linen merchant, of four bank notes together with all his silver coins, his great coat and umbrella, after they all had shared a few beers and a half glass of whiskey at Mr Mann's public house in Castledawson, County Derry. In the transportation register Wilson Cornwall's crime was classed as highway robbery. Prior to transportation, Wilson Cornwall was held in the County Jail on Bishop Street in the city of Derry.

To entice the Irish emigrant to Australia, assisted passage was introduced. Lists of these immigrants date from 1828 and the information in them is very comprehensive. For example, in 1864 Thomas Connolly arrived at Sydney on board the ship *Serocco*. Thomas, aged 29, was a Roman Catholic and a policeman from Ballygar in County Galway. He could read and write, and his parents were Michael and Ellen Connolly, also of Ballygar. Thus, with this one entry you have all the information you need to trace the Connolly in Ireland.

Birth, marriage and death certificates, likewise, provide an abundance of information. For example, from the New South Wales death certificate of Sarah Heathwood, who died on 3 April 1936, aged 94, we can deduce the following information: Sarah was born in Ardarragh townland in Newry Parish, County Down around 1842; in 1867, aged 25 years, she married William Heathwood in County Roscommon; her children, John born c. 1868, Robert 1869, Annie 1871, Richard 1874, and William 1876, were all born in Ireland; in 1877 the family immigrated to Queensland where another son, Joseph, was born in 1879. Sarah was buried on 4th April 1936 in the Presbyterian cemetery at Casino, New South Wales. A full family history can, therefore, be gleaned from this one certificate.

Gravestone inscriptions should also be searched. In the Catholic cemetery at Hartley, New South Wales, a tombstone erected by the police of Western District records that Thomas Madden, a constable born in County Mayo, was accidently shot dead at Pilpit Hill on 30 April 1867, aged 30.

NEW ZEALAND

Passenger lists in New Zealand, as in Australia, were kept at the port of arrival. The earliest are those for the New Zealand Company vessels, arriving at the ports of Wellington, Nelson, New Plymouth and Otago. These lists date from 1840 and provide the emigrant's name, age, occupation, wife's age and children's ages and sex. New Zealand became a British colony in 1840, when she was annexed to New South Wales. Passenger lists, therefore, go back to the earliest beginnings of the colony.

Before 1840, New Zealand had a very small European population. According to the *Derry Journal* of 18 February 1840, "With but few exceptions, the white population was composed of outcasts of Great Britain – runaway convicts, swindlers and thieves from New South Wales and Van Dieman's Land."

From 1853, New Zealand was administered by provincial governments at Canterbury, Wellington, Nelson, Auckland and Otago. Each province compiled passenger lists of varying quality.

Unfortunately, in both New Zealand and Australia, census records were destroyed once the relevant statistical information had been extracted from them.

Civil registration of births and deaths commenced in 1848, but marriages were not recorded until 1855. In terms of identifying the Irish origins of an ancestor, death certificates are an extremely valuable source, especially after 1876. From that year the place of birth, the parent's names and the date and place of marriage of the deceased were recorded. Marriage certificates from 1880 are equally useful as they give the birthplace and parents' names of both bride and groom.

Parish registers of baptisms, marriages and burials, held locally by the clergymen, should be consulted for details of births, marriages and deaths before the commencement of civil registration.

UNITED STATES OF AMERICA

A New York genealogist, B-Ann Moorhouse, made use of federal and state censuses, marriage and death records, naturalization records, directories, passenger lists, probate records, cemetery inscriptions and death notices in newspapers to research 400 Irish-born and their descendants who resided in Brooklyn, New York during the 19th century. Regarding clues to place of origin in Ireland, she found death notices in the local Brooklyn newspapers of the time to be of most value, as they consistently gave the exact place of origin of the Irish-born. In another case, the will of William Ferguson, dated 1873, in mentioning a farm his sister had left to him in Ballygarvey in Rathaspick Parish, County Westmeath, identified the Irish origins of this Brooklyn merchant.

The U.S. has comprehensive passenger lists for ships arriving from 1820, but unfortunately, they provide only two clues relating to the origin of the emigrant – the port of departure of the ship and the nationality of the passenger. This is of limited value when it is realized that the vast majority of Irish emigrants in the 19th century sailed from Liverpool. The lists, however, give the name, occupation and age of the emigrant. It was not until the Immigration Act of 1893 that the former address in Ireland of an emigrant was recorded.

Prior to 1890, no official registers of passengers leaving Irish ports were kept except for a brief period, 1803-1806. Among the business records of two Derry firms, J & J Cooke for the years 1847 to 1867, and William McCorkell & Co., 1863 to 1871, passenger lists recording the residence of 27,495 Irish emigrants have survived. The major destinations of the passengers carried by these firms were New York and Philadelphia in the U.S., and Quebec and Saint John, New Brunswick in Canada. The Ordnance Survey map compilers recorded the names, ages, religion and townland addresses of emigrants for many parishes in Counties Antrim and Derry for a few years during the period 1833 to 1839. Again, Canada and the U.S. were the major destinations of these emigrants. These sources of Irish passenger lists have been transcribed, indexed and published by the Genealogical Publishing Company of Baltimore.

In colonial America the Land Patent Books of Virginia, the registers of indentured servants in Pennsylvania, and petitions for land grants in Maryland and South Carolina identify many recently arrived immigrants.

A census has been taken every ten years in the U.S. since 1790, and from 1850 the returns provide the country of birth and age of all members of the household, not just the head of household.

Tombstone inscriptions should be sought out. In St. Mary's Cemetery in Lee, Massachusetts, the following inscription can be found: "John Dooley, a native of the town of Leabeg, parish of Ferbane, King's County, died August 14 1863 aged 53 years." King's County is now renamed County Offaly.

Naturalization records are another useful source. On April 1839, for example, John Austin, aged 26, giving his place of birth as County Leitrim, declared his intention before Franklin County Court at St. Albans, Vermont to become a U.S. citizen.

CANADA

As pre-1865 passenger lists for Canada are rare, this makes the business records of Cooke and McCorkell and the emigrant lists in the Ordnance Survey memoirs (both described previously) very valuable indeed. Lists of passenger arrivals at Halifax and Quebec were kept from 1865.

In 1871 the Province of New Brunswick, with 35% of its population of Irish origin, was one of the most Irish jurisdictions outside of Ireland. In contrast to the United States the greatest numbers of Irish came to Canada in the pre-Famine period. The New Brunswick Irish Portal at **https://archives.gnb.ca/Irish/databases_en.html** includes a database of pre-1840 passenger lists, which name 10,451 immigrants (9,721 from Ireland, 410 from England and 320 from Scotland) who arrived at New Brunswick ports, namely: Saint John in 1816, 1833, 1834 and 1838; St. Andrews in 1837 and 1838; and Bathurst in 1837.

In 1895, after it was noted that 40% of all passengers arriving in Canada were actually bound for the U.S., a system of joint inspection of immigrants coming overland from Canada was established. From 1847, the two ports of Portland and Falmouth, Maine were becoming increasingly popular as ports of entry for Irish immigrants coming down from Quebec and the Maritime Provinces to the U.S. In these cases, therefore, Irish immigrants leaving Canada for the U.S. will be noted.

In the absence of passenger lists the best hope of linking an ancestor to his place of origin in Ireland may lie in the identification of a marriage entry of a newly arrived immigrant in a church register. Frequently, the marriage registers give the county of birth in Ireland, and occasionally, the exact place of origin of bride and groom. In the years 1801 to 1845, for example, the weddings of 3,000 Irish immigrants, giving their parents' names and native parishes, were recorded in Halifax, Nova Scotia.

Land grants can be extremely useful in identifying recent immigrants. To obtain land from the colonial government and, after 1867 from the Provincial authorities, a settler had to make a formal application, known as a petition, in which details on place of origin, date of arrival in Canada, name of wife and children and their ages are often given. There exists a computerized Land Records Index for the years 1780 to 1914 with two alphabetical listings, one by applicant's name and one by township.

Gravestone inscriptions can prove very enlightening. For example, in Barkerville cemetery in Barkerville, British Columbia, one of the tombstones reads, "In memory of Patrick McKenna, native of Duleek, County Meath, Ireland, Died June 2, 1914 aged 59."

Death notices in newspapers should also be sought out. *The Herald*, the local newspaper of Charlottetown, Prince Edward Island, on 3 July 1867 carried the following death notice, "On Monday June 3rd at his residence, Monaghan Settlement Lot 36, James Trainor, aged 80 years. The deceased was a native of the parish of Donah, townland of Strawmore, County Monaghan, Ireland and emigrated to this island in the year 1835, May he rest in peace."

GREAT BRITAIN

Civil registration of births, marriages and deaths began in England and Wales in 1837 and in Scotland in 1855. Despite providing much genealogical information of great value, they give no clue to the former residence of those who were born in Ireland. The marriage entries in church records, however, can provide the Irish origins of bride and groom. For example, the register of St. Vincent de Paul in Liverpool on 4 June 1862 records the marriage of Joseph Edward Hughes of Sligo to Sarah Quin of 13 Moore Place, London Road, Liverpool.

From 1841, census returns in both England and Scotland list all members of the household, together with their ages and occupations. Furthermore, they will identify those people who were born in Ireland. In Scotland, from 1851, the specific town or parish of birth is given.

Gravestone inscriptions and death notices in newspapers will probably provide the best means of identifying a more precise Irish address of an ancestor. In Clifton Parish churchyard, Bristol, there can be found the following gravestone inscription: "Mary Clutterbuck of Derryhusker, County Tipperary, Ireland, died 17 December 1847, aged 99 years." And in the *Bristol Journal* of Saturday, 21 January 1837, the following death notice was reported: "January 14 at Royal York Crescent, Clifton, Robert Eyre Purdon Coote Esqr., of Ballyclough, County Cork,"

Hopefully, all these examples show that much can be done in the home country to identify as precisely as possible the names of ancestors who emigrated from Ireland; their age, so that an approximate date of birth can be estimated; where they lived in Ireland and their religious denomination. Armed with this information, you can then begin to conduct research through Irish record sources and begin to plan your trip to Ireland to walk in "the footsteps of your ancestors."

FIRST STEPS

The first, and perhaps the most crucial, step in compiling your family tree is probably the one most people neglect: namely the quizzing of relations and family friends. It is too often assumed that genealogy means looking through dusty parish registers that haven't seen the light of day in years or walking through overgrown cemeteries in search of an ancestor's gravestone; in other words, a total reliance on the written word. People who do this are not only missing out on a vital source of information but also on one of the joys of genealogy. The information and anecdotes relatives can provide help bring the family tree to life and can also provide much-needed clues for its construction. The oral tradition within the family circle is of immense value.

Having made the decision to research your family tree, now is the time to get in touch with those relatives you haven't seen in ages. Parents, grandparents, uncles and aunts should all be questioned. Names, places, dates and any anecdotes, no matter how unlikely or inaccurate you might think them to be, associated with all branches of your family tree should be recorded. In genealogy, you never know when a piece of information that seemed irrelevant might, on reflection, suggest a line of enquiry. There are many instances where family folklore, passed down through the generations, extends beyond what is written in historical records or captured in databases.

The memories and knowledge of the elderly should not be underestimated. The McCook family story, as described in the first chapter, was built on the knowledge of 87-year-old Robert Graham. In my case, I had two 80-year-old aunts who could remember as young girls sitting with their grandmother, listening to the stories she told them. It was through their recollections that I was able to trace the English origins of the Metcalfes of Lurgan, County Armagh. They were able to tell me that George Metcalfe, my great-grandfather, came from Headington in Oxfordshire in the 19th century to set up a poultry business in Lurgan. The registers of Headington Parish church confirmed this. On 12 April 1840, George was baptized, his parents being George Metcalfe and Mary Wake. According to the 1841 census, George Metcalfe senior was a blacksmith and a gun maker and the family lived at Church Lane in Headington. Without the oral tradition, the identification of George Metcalfe's birthplace would have been a more difficult task. The Irish 1901 census return for George, however, giving his age as 60 and his birthplace as Oxfordshire, does provide sufficient information to search English civil registers of births, which commence from 1837 – the moral being, if one avenue closes its doors to you, search for another.

In one interesting case, a lady who contacted me was attempting to trace her own name, which was a rather unusual one, Tarleton. The oral tradition passed down in the family is that the Tarletons came to County Offaly (then known as King's County) from Liverpool in the 16th century. Tarleton is indeed a Lancashire name, as the surname is derived from a place of that name in that county. Furthermore, history records when Mary Tudor came to the throne of England in 1553, lands that had been confiscated from the O'Mores and O'Connors of Counties Leix and Offaly were planted by settlers from England. These counties were then renamed Queen's County and King's County. It seems the Tarletons came over with this plantation. The mid-19th-century Griffith's Valuation and early-19th-century Tithe Applotment Books for County Offaly seem to confirm this, inasmuch as in the early-19th-century Tarleton households could be found in Ballykean, Geashill, Killoughy and Kilmanaghan parishes, with a concentration in the parish of Geashill, especially.

In addition to oral tradition, a search should be made through family papers to unearth old photographs, newspaper clippings with perhaps an obituary, letters, or even a family Bible with its own family tree within. Until you look, you never know what useful information may be lurking in the back of a cupboard or hiding in a box in the attic.

You will soon find that you have amassed a lot of information that needs to be organized to prevent it from becoming unwieldy. The simplest and most effective method is a pre-printed family history chart on which you can record details of direct line ancestors. A family history chart for the recording of up to four generations is enclosed with this book. Make as many photocopies of it as you require. Against "Family Tree," enter the surname of the family line being traced. Against "You," enter your own name or the name of the ancestor being traced. Then fill in the full names of parents, grandparents and great-grandparents. For each name enter their date and place of birth, marriage and death. Information that is unknown is simply left blank, thus highlighting those areas where further research is needed. The chart will be constantly updated as new information comes to light.

Alternatively, you can download and print, free of charge or to purchase, family tree charts on which to record your family history discoveries; simply search an internet search engine such as Google, **www.google.com**, with keywords "Family Tree Charts."

The pre-printed family history chart is ideal for those recording all family lines, but it offers no space for detailing collateral ancestors, i.e. the brothers and sisters of direct line ancestors and their descendants. This is easily overcome by drawing up your own family history chart in which there are no limitations to its size. For example, on a roll of paper with dimensions of 15 feet by 2 feet deep a relative has drawn up a family tree that identifies all offspring from my great-grandparents George Mitchell and Margaret Jane Patton and their eleven children.

The conventions in drawing up your own family history chart are straightforward. Start at the top of the page with the ancestor whose descendants you want to record and link them to their spouse with the recognized marriage symbol of "=". From this marriage symbol, draw a vertical line to join a horizontal line whose length is determined by the number of children attached to it by other short vertical lines. The same procedure is followed for any other marriages amongst these children. Children should be listed in order of birth, but in some circumstances it is advantageous to change the order so as to fit the requirements of your chart design. The following standard symbols and abbreviations should be used: "b." for born, "c." about, "m." married, "d." died, "?" if uncertain of accuracy of information, and blank spaces for information that is not yet known. An example of such a family history chart, drawn up to present the McCook family history described previously, is shown below.

Note how people of the same generation are kept on the same level. In this case two sets of cousins are displayed with John's sons being born in New Zealand and Archibald's children in Ireland. The great advantage with such a chart is that you choose what families to highlight. In our example it is the families of Archibald and John.

With this type of family history chart, it is perhaps best to draw up a rough draft to ensure all issue you want to include can be accommodated, as such charts lose their visual attractiveness and clarity if you continually add to them. Our chart would need to be redesigned if we wanted to include the children of Robert, the youngest son of Alexander McCook. For those with artistic flair, their family history charts could become the focus of considerable attention and envy!

FAMILY TREE

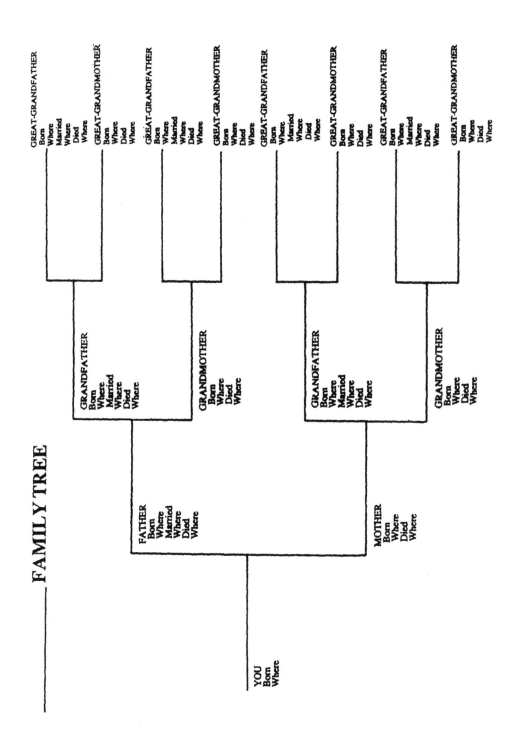

YOU
Born
Where

FATHER
Born
Where
Married
Where
Died
Where

MOTHER
Born
Where
Died
Where

GRANDFATHER
Born
Where
Married
Where
Died
Where

GRANDMOTHER
Born
Where
Died
Where

GRANDFATHER
Born
Where
Married
Where
Died
Where

GRANDMOTHER
Born
Where
Died
Where

GREAT-GRANDFATHER
Born
Where
Married
Where
Died
Where

GREAT-GRANDMOTHER
Born
Where
Died
Where

GREAT-GRANDFATHER
Born
Where
Married
Where
Died
Where

GREAT-GRANDMOTHER
Born
Where
Died
Where

GREAT-GRANDFATHER
Born
Where
Married
Where
Died
Where

GREAT-GRANDMOTHER
Born
Where
Died
Where

GREAT-GRANDFATHER
Born
Where
Married
Where
Died
Where

GREAT-GRANDMOTHER
Born
Where
Died
Where

McCOOK FAMILY TREE - IRELAND, AUSTRALIA AND NEW ZEALAND

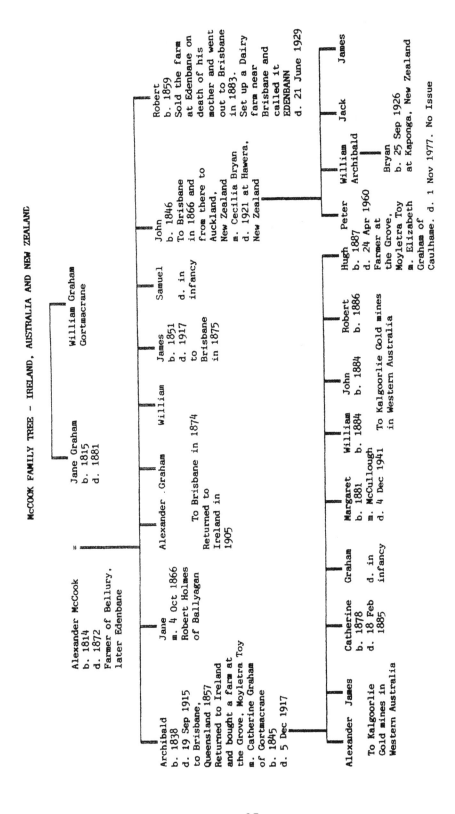

Alexander McCook
b. 1814
d. 1872
Farmer of Bellury,
later Edenbane

=

Jane Graham
b. 1815
d. 1881

William Graham
Gortmacrane

Archibald
b. 1838
d. 19 Sep 1915
to Brisbane,
Queensland 1857
Returned to Ireland
and bought a farm at
the Grove, Moyletra Toy
m. Catherine Graham
of Gortmacrane
b. 1845
d. 5 Dec 1917

Jane
m. 4 Oct 1866
Robert Holmes
of Ballyagan

Alexander Graham

William

To Brisbane in 1874
Returned to
Ireland in
1905

Samuel
d. in
infancy

James
b. 1851
d. 1917
to
Brisbane
in 1875

Robert
b. 1859
Sold the farm
at Edenbane on
death of his
mother and went
out to Brisbane
in 1883.
Set up a Dairy
farm near
Brisbane and
called it
EDENBANN
d. 21 June 1929

John
b. 1846
To Brisbane
in 1866 and
from there to
Auckland,
New Zealand
m. Cecilia Bryan
d. 1921 at Hawera.
New Zealand

Alexander James

To Kalgoorlie
Gold mines in
Western Australia

Catherine
b. 1878
d. 18 Feb
1885

Graham
d. in
infancy

Margaret
b. 1881
m. McCullough
d. 4 Dec 1941

William
b. 1884
To Kalgoorlie Gold mines
in Western Australia

John
b. 1884

Robert
b. 1886

Hugh Peter
b. 1887
d. 24 Apr 1960
Farmer at
the Grove,
Moyletra Toy
m. Elizabeth
Graham of
Caulhame. d. 1 Nov 1977. No Issue

William
Archibald

Jack

James

Bryan
b. 25 Sep 1926
at Kaponga, New Zealand
d. 1 Nov 1977. No Issue

25

You could also explore building family history charts with genealogy software packages, such as: Family Tree Builder from MyHeritage (**www.familytreebuilder.com**); AncestralQuest (AQ) family tree software (**www.ancquest.com**); or Family Tree Maker 2019 (FTM), which is one of the world's most popular genealogy software packages (**www.mackiev.com**).

WikiTree (**www.wikitree.com**), a free website, encourages family historians to collaborate to build a single worldwide family tree. To date, over 650,000 family historians have created 22 million ancestral profiles, which can then be used to research your own family tree.

By the time you've visited or contacted your relatives, located any old family history documents, and recorded all this information on family history charts, you should have built up an outline family tree detailing names, locations and dates of Irish-born ancestors. Only now should you consider searching the seven major record sources outlined in the next chapter to confirm, fill in and extend your family tree.

Sources

MAJOR RECORD SOURCES

I have found, since I first started work as a genealogist in 1982, that the seven record sources examined in this section will enable you to build up a detailed family tree stretching back six or seven generations. These records are civil registers, parish registers, gravestone inscriptions, wills, 1901 and 1911 census returns, Griffith's Valuation and Tithe Applotment Books. To make the text lest cluttered, fuller details on the administrative divisions and record offices, which will be constantly referred to in this section, are contained in the Insights and Strategies section at the back of the book. Refer to this section whenever you feel you need more detail. For each record source is included a description, detail on how to make best use of the record, and suggestions for using the information it contains to further your research.

CIVIL REGISTERS OF BIRTH, MARRIAGES AND DEATHS

Civil registration in Ireland of births, deaths and Roman Catholic marriages didn't commence until January 1864. Non-Catholic marriages, however, were subject to registration from April 1845. For the purpose of registration, Ireland was divided into about 800 registrars' districts, which were grouped into 140 poor law unions (also known as Superintendent Registrars' districts). The registrar of the union was responsible for collecting the registrations made by his district registrars and returning the lot to the Registrar General in Dublin, where complete indexes covering the whole country were compiled.

The detail included in birth, marriage and death certificates, together with their associated indexes, help to make this source an ideal starting point in researching ancestors who were born, married or died after the commencement of civil registration.

A birth certificate provides the name, date of birth and place of birth of the child, together with the father's name, occupation and residence, and the mother's name and maiden name.

A marriage certificate gives the names, ages, occupations and residences of the bride and groom, together with the names and occupations of their fathers. The date and place of marriage and the names of two witnesses are also included.

A death certificate gives the deceased's name, age, occupation, date of death, place of death and cause of death.

The certificates, therefore, vary in the amount and usefulness of information provided. Death certificates offer the minimum of information and, in many cases, are only useful as a means to get an approximate date of birth of an ancestor, from the age given at death. A birth certificate, on the other hand, provides detail on three ancestors, namely father, mother and child. A marriage certificate is perhaps the most useful, as it provides information on four direct ancestors and two branches of the family tree, i.e. the bride's and groom's lines. By giving the addresses of both bride and groom at the time of their marriage, it may be possible to identify two ancestral homes.

Civil birth, marriage and death certificates were indexed; the early indexes were compiled annually, while the later ones (from 1878) were arranged by quarter year. They were arranged in alphabetical order by surname and then by Christian name.

In the time period 1864 to 1902 and 1928 to 1966, the indexes to civil birth, marriage and death registers list the year (quarter year from 1878) of registration of the event, the name, the poor law union in which the event was registered, and the volume and page number of the register in which the event will be found. The indexes for 1903 to 1927 provide additional information such as the date of the event, mother's maiden name in birth indexes, spouse's surname in marriage indexes, and age and marital condition of deceased in death indexes.

Owing to the limited information provided in the original indexes, it would be very difficult to identify an ancestor, especially one with a common surname, without fairly precise information to the date and location of the event. Furthermore, the only guidance to the address is the poor law union name in which the event was registered. This means, for example, that the only address information provided in the indexes to events registered in County Wicklow are the five poor law union names of Baltinglass, Naas, Rathdown, Rathdrum and Shillelagh.

To make effective use of these indexes, therefore, you ideally need to identify the union or unions associated with your ancestors. You can do this by making use of a book called *The General Alphabetical Index to the Townlands and Towns, Parishes and Baronies of Ireland*, better known as "The Townland Index." This book will identify the poor law union for all of Ireland's 60,462 townlands. You can also search the Townland Index online, together with street listings from Dublin, Cork and Belfast cities, to pinpoint county, civil parish and poor law union locations for more than 65,000 placenames in Ireland, by using the "placename" search option at **www.johngrenham.com/places**.

Irish "historic" civil records, i.e. births over 100 years old, marriages over 75 years, and deaths over 50 years, are searchable online. The more recent records will be held in the appropriate General Register Office, i.e. General Register Office of Ireland in Roscommon and General Register Office for Northern Ireland in Belfast.

Irish civil records of births, marriages and deaths can now be searched and viewed at **www.irishgenealogy.ie**. On searching the index, which returns name, event type, year and name of Superintendent Registrar's District, a pdf of the full register page in which that birth, marriage or death certificate appears can be downloaded by selecting "image." At present, images are available for Births 1864-1919, Marriages 1845-1944 and Deaths 1878-1969. Further register images of Deaths 1864-1877 will follow later.

This website's civil records cover the entire island of Ireland up to and including 1921. From 1922, it does not hold records registered in the six counties of Northern Ireland. However, you can search "historic" civil records of births, marriages and deaths for Northern Ireland at GRONI online and, by purchasing credits, view births (over 100 years old), marriages (over 75 years old) and deaths (over 50 years old) on the website of the General Register Office of Northern Ireland at **www.nidirect.gov.uk/services/go-groni-online**.

Examples of a birth, marriage and death certificate, together with the appropriate entries in the indexes are shown overleaf. They demonstrate very nicely how a family tree can be built up using a series of certificates.

BIRTH CERTIFICATE

Index: Mitchell Samuel Patton, Londonderry   Vol 17 page 217 Year 1868

1868 Births registered in the District of Killea in the Union of Londonderry in the County of Donegal

No	Date and Place of Birth	Name	Sex	Name and Surname and Dwelling Place of Father	Name and Surname & Maiden Surname of Mother	Rank or Profession of Father	Signature, Qualification and Residence of Informant	When Registered
	Twenty second September 1868 Colehill All Saints	Samuel	Male	George Mitchell Colehill	Margaret Jane Mitchell Formerly Patton	School Master	George Mitchell Father Colehill	3rd Oct 1868

MARRIAGE CERTIFICATE

Index: Mitchell George. Newry   Vol 8 Page 510 Year 1853

      Patton Margaret Jane, Newry   Vol 8 Page 510 Year 1853

1853 Marriage solemnised at Balleek Church in the Parish of Balleek in the County of Armagh

No	When married	Name and Surname	Age	Condition	Rank or profession	Residence at the time of marriage	Father's name and Surname	Rank or Profession of father
	8th January 1853	George Mitchell	of age	Bachelor	Schoolmaster	All Saints. Donegal	George Mitchell	School-master
		Margaret Jane Patton	of age	Spinster	-----	Carrickananny	William Patton	Farmer

Married in the Parish church of Balleek according to the Rites and Ceremonies of the United Church of England and Ireland by me

                                             Charles Crossler

                 in the presence of us   Henry Devlin

                                            John Patton

DEATH CERTIFICATE

Index: 1901 June Quarter Mitchell George, Magherafelt   Vol 1 page 601

1901 Deaths registered in the District of Maghera in the Union of Magherafelt in the County of Londonderry

No	Date and Place of Death	Name and Surname	Sex	Condition	Age last Birthday	Rank, Profession or occupation	Certified cause of death and duration of illness	Signature, qualification and residence of informant	When registered
	1901 Fourth April Normeal	George Mitchell	Male	Widower	73 years	Clerk of Petty Sessions (Retired)	Age and Influenza fourteen days certified	John Mitchell son Normeal	13th April 1901

The following family tree can be drawn up from the three certificates:

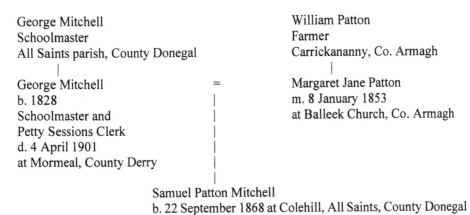

George Mitchell
Schoolmaster
All Saints parish, County Donegal
|
George Mitchell   =
b. 1828
Schoolmaster and
Petty Sessions Clerk
d. 4 April 1901
at Mormeal, County Derry

William Patton
Farmer
Carrickananny, Co. Armagh
|
Margaret Jane Patton
m. 8 January 1853
at Balleek Church, Co. Armagh

Samuel Patton Mitchell
b. 22 September 1868 at Colehill, All Saints, County Donegal

The information contained in birth, marriage and death certificates provides many clues on which to base further research. In our example, the following steps could be followed up: the search of relevant church registers at Balleek and Colehill for Patton and Mitchell baptisms, respectively; a visit to graveyards around Colehill, Carrickananny and Mormeal; the identification of George Mitchell's will, as we know he died in 1901; a search of the 1901 census returns for Mormeal, as this census was taken just a few days before George died; and a look through Griffith's Valuation for Mitchells at Colehill and Pattons at Carrickananny.

CHURCH REGISTERS OF BAPTISMS, MARRIAGES AND BURIALS

Before civil registration, birth, marriage and death details of an ancestor will have to be found in baptism, marriage and burial entries in church registers. The identification of an ancestor in these records will require careful preparation. Unlike civil registers there is no national index to church registers, but the rewards from using this source are well worth the effort. Church registers, like civil registers, supply enough information to build and confirm family linkages.

A baptism entry can provide the name of the child, date of baptism, date of birth, parents' names, parents' address (by townland), father's occupation, and names of sponsors (particularly in Roman Catholic registers).

A marriage entry can provide the names of the bride and groom, their places of residence, date of marriage, parents' names, and names of witnesses.

A burial entry can provide the name and residence of the deceased, burial date and place, and age of the deceased. In the case of children, the names of parents may be included.

It must be emphasized that dates of commencement and quality of information in church registers vary widely from parish to parish and from denomination to denomination. For example, in Derry city, the earliest baptismal register is that of St. Columb's Church of Ireland Cathedral, which dates from 1642, but the earliest Presbyterian and Roman Catholic baptismal registers for the city commence in 1815 and 1823, respectively.

Before seeking out church records you will need to know where your ancestors lived and their religious denomination, as Ireland has a complex parish structure. The Church of Ireland and

Roman Catholic churches have an all-Ireland parish structure, the former because of its privileged position, before 1870, as the Established Church, and the latter because of its numerical strength.

The Church of Ireland parish largely coincides with the boundaries of the civil parish and retains the civil parish name, while the Catholic parish does not necessarily correspond with either the names or boundaries of the civil parishes. The Roman Catholic Church, owing to the reformation of the 16th century, had to adapt itself to a new parish structure centered on towns and villages. The Presbyterian church doesn't have a parish structure as such, with the congregations generally forming where there was sufficient demand from local Presbyterian families. In those areas with a high Presbyterian population, there could be many Presbyterian meeting houses. For example, the civil parish of Ballymore in County Armagh had six Presbyterian congregations by the middle of the 19th century. By contrast, in County Wicklow, with 57 civil parishes, there was only one Presbyterian congregation – at Bray. The other Protestant dissenting denominations, such as Methodists, Baptists, Congregationalists and Quakers, formed where there were enough like-minded people.

Realistic genealogical research, in the absence of indexes and databases, generally requires knowledge of the parish in which your ancestor lived. Researchers can identify Ireland's network of civil parishes at **www.johngrenham.com/places/civil_index.php** and Roman Catholic parishes at **www.johngrenham.com/places/rcmap_index.php** by selecting county of interest on the displayed map of Ireland.

A Topographical Dictionary of Ireland by Samuel Lewis, published in 1837, is a useful source for identifying the churches of each denomination located within each civil parish. Arranged in alphabetical order by parishes, towns and villages, this book can be viewed online at **www.libraryireland.com/topog/placeindex.php**.

By using *A New Genealogical Atlas of Ireland* (2nd edition, Brian Mitchell, Genealogical Publishing Company, Baltimore, 2002) civil parish locations can be translated into Church of Ireland parishes, Roman Catholic parishes and Presbyterian congregations (in province of Ulster). Presbyterian congregations in Ireland are very much associated with the nine counties of the northern province of Ulster.

After identifying the religious affiliation of your ancestor and their residence, you need to identify what church registers exist for that area and their dates of commencement. In the case of the Church of Ireland, many of their early registers do not survive; of 1,006 pre-1870 registers deposited in the Public Record Office, Dublin, all but four were burned in the fire there in 1922. Despite the fire, many registers of great age have survived. For example, in County Dublin 17 Church of Ireland registers with commencement dates between 1619 and 1699 and 20 between 1700 and 1799 survive.

One feature of the Presbyterian church is the concentration of congregations within relatively small areas. Doctrinal differences and disagreements over choice of minister often divided the original congregation and led to the creation of a new one. This 19th-century growth of Presbyterian congregations in Ulster may mean two or three registers need to be examined, even if you know the exact area your ancestor lived in. It is also very possible for the baptism, marriage and burial records of Protestant dissenters to be within the registers of the Church of Ireland, as for centuries the Established Church (i.e. Church of Ireland) claimed the right to administer baptism, marriage and burial ceremonies to all Protestants.

In the case of the Roman Catholic church, the Penal Laws resulted in the late erection of chapels in many parishes and the late commencement of many registers. Of the 41 Catholic parishes serving the 52 civil parishes of County Donegal, 29 of them have registers that don't commence until after 1850. The Catholic registers, however, in the bigger towns and cities can be of an early date. There are baptism and marriage records for Wexford town dating back to 1671. Waterford has four parishes whose registers date back to the 1700s.

By using *A Guide to Irish Parish Registers* (Brian Mitchell, Genealogical Publishing Company, Baltimore, 1988) civil parish locations can be translated into a listing of surviving church registers of all denominations and their commencement dates.

There is no national index to Irish church registers. To date, only the county-based genealogy centers have attempted any large scale, systematic indexing of church registers in their localities, and these can be searched at **www.rootsireland.ie**. For example, County Derry database compiled by Derry Genealogy contains pre-1900 registers of 26 Roman Catholic parishes, 24 Church of Ireland parishes and 35 Presbyterian congregations; while County Mayo database compiled by North Mayo Heritage Centre and South Mayo Family Research Centre consists of pre-1900 registers of 55 Roman Catholic parishes, 23 Church of Ireland parishes and 9 Presbyterian congregations.

As the search facility on this website, i.e. **www.rootsireland.ie**, is very flexible it means that you should be able to determine if any entries of interest to your family history are held on this database. You can either search across all counties or search a particular county. For example, if you are searching for the baptism/birth of a child you can narrow the search down by year, range of years, names of parents and by parish of baptism/district of birth. Marriage searches can be filtered by year, range of years, name of spouse, names of parents and parish/district of marriage.

Although RootsIreland is the largest online source of Irish church register transcripts, it must be emphasized that a failure to find relevant birth/marriage entries in this database doesn't mean that the events you are looking for didn't happen in Ireland. It simply means that they are not recorded in the database; for example, they may be recorded in a record source which doesn't survive for the time period of interest or in a source that has not been computerized.

A database, of course, is only as good as the information it holds – if data is entered incorrectly or just simply does not exist in the first place, there is nothing a website can do to rectify this. The absence of relevant records is a well-known problem in Irish genealogy as many records were either destroyed or simply not kept until quite late on. It is quite possible, for example, that the baptism you seek occurred before its written confirmation in a surviving church register.

Since each county center, whose records are accessible at **www.rootsireland.ie**, employs a genealogist, with knowledge of both family history sources and local history, it makes sense to contact them to see if they can assist you; for example, to answer queries you may have about placenames, surname origins, sources to search, record offices to visit or research recommendations. Contact details for each county center are clearly displayed by selecting the county of interest at **www.rootsireland.ie/map**.

The Representative Church Body (RCB) Library in Churchtown, Dublin (**https://www.ireland.anglican.org/about/rcb-library**) is the place of deposit for Church of

Ireland registers and today the RCB Library's parish collections number 1,114. A comprehensive list of Church of Ireland Parish Registers, which is color-coded to identify what survives, can be viewed at the following website: **www.ireland.anglican.org/cmsfiles/ pdf/AboutUs/library/registers/ParishRegisters/PARISHREGISTERS.pdf**. This list also includes live links to online parish register sources. The two major websites holding indexes to Church of Ireland parish registers are **www.rootsireland.ie** and **www.irishgenealogy.ie**.

A list of Church of Ireland parish registers held on microfilm, which can be accessed in National Archives of Ireland, is available at the website **www.nationalarchives.ie/wp-content/uploads/2018/02/CofIMicrofilms.pdf**.

In September 2018 funding was secured by RCB library to digitize Church of Ireland parish registers, and ultimately, the digitized records will be indexed and made available at **www.irishgenealogy.ie**. At present, researchers can search, free of charge, at this website, Church of Ireland parish registers for counties Carlow and Kerry and Dublin city; and Roman Catholic parish registers of County Kerry, Dublin city and west and south Cork (i.e. parishes in Dioceses of Kerry and Cork and Ross except most of Cork city).

By visiting the website of the National Library of Ireland at **https://registers.nli.ie**, you can examine pre-1880 Roman Catholic registers for most parishes of Ireland, either by entering the parish name or by selecting county and then parish of interest on the map of Ireland. On selecting a parish you can then browse through a scanned copy of pre-1880 registers that until recently were only accessible on microfilm in the National Library of Ireland. Furthermore, an index to these digitized images of pre-1880 Roman Catholic Irish parish registers can be searched at **www.ancestry.com** and **www.findmypast.com**.

Microfilm copy of church registers of all denominations for most parishes in the nine counties of Ulster can be examined, at no charge, in the Public Record Office of Northern Ireland in Belfast. Their *Guide To Church Records*, which can be accessed on their website at **www.nidirect.gov.uk/publications/proni-guide-church-records**, lists, in alphabetical order by civil parish, church registers of all denominations and their commencement dates, together with their microfilm reference details.

Having decided on a register to search, whether it is the original register or a microfilm or digitized copy, you will have to resist the impulse to glance quickly through the pages, stopping only briefly at those surnames that you think might belong to your ancestors. The registers, especially of a later date, may be tabulated and the information written in the appropriate columns, neatly and legibly. But often the information is simply written, and not too clearly at that, in sentence form. The implications for the impatient will be to overlook the very entry you are looking for.

With handwritten records there is always the possibility of misreading surnames. Complicating matters further are the numerous spelling variations to be found of the same name. Uniformity in spelling surnames is really a phenomenon of the 20th century. The clergy, in entering relevant details, often had to write down names based on pronunciation, as many people could not write down or spell their name. The diversity was perpetuated by the fact that there were no recognized standards for spelling surnames.

On identifying a likely name in a register that has a slightly different spelling from the name you are looking for, ask yourself if it is merely a spelling variation of the same name or a completely different name. The Thurles Parish indexing project in County Tipperary found, for example, that it was often difficult to distinguish Phelan from Whelan, Bourke from Rourke and Kelly from Kiely in their registers. The anglicization of the Gaelic can also cause problems. For example, the surname Flood can be a translation of Gaelic *tuile*, meaning flood, which was also anglicized as Tully. In the Thurles registers, both names, Tully and Flood, frequently occur.

The patience and care taken in searching church registers is well worth it. You may be very fortunate and be able to follow successive generations back in time:

SHANKILL PARISH, COUNTY ARMAGH (CHURCH OF IRELAND)

Baptism Register
11 July 1824 Henry of parents Henry and May Corner of Lurgan

Marriage Register
23 April 1844 Henry Corner of Toberhuney in this parish, bachelor and Letitia Mathews of Cornreaney in the Parish of Donaghcloney, Spinster. By license

A family tree can be drawn:

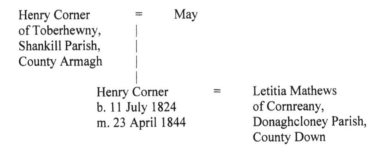

Like civil registers, because of their similar nature, the information from baptism, marriage and burial registers on names, dates, places and family connections can provide pointers to other record sources to search. In our example, the marriage register identified two ancestral homes, namely Toberhewny townland in Shankill Parish, County Armagh and Cornreany townland in Donaghcloney parish, County Down. The local graveyards can, therefore, be identified and visited. We can quickly search the tithe books, Griffith's Valuation and 1901 and 1911 census returns for the townlands of Toberhewny and Cornreany to identify Corner and Mathews households, respectively. These two townlands are in the poor law union of Lurgan, so the indexes to civil registers could be searched for Corner and Mathews' birth, marriage and death entries recorded against "Civil Registration District" of Lurgan.

To conclude this section, let's return to the family tree of George Mitchell, which was built with a strong foundation of civil birth, marriage and death registers, to see how we can use church registers to continue growing the tree:

BALLYNASCREEN PARISH, COUNTY DERRY (CHURCH OF IRELAND)

Baptism Register
Baptised: 7 March 1813 Jane of George Mitchell of Cahore
Baptised: 14 January 1819 Elizabeth of George and Elizabeth Mitchell
Born: 2 May 1827 Baptised: 5 May 1827 George of George and Elizabeth Mitchell

Burial Register
Buried: 28 October 1857 George Mitchell of Cahore, age 70
Buried: 3 March 1851 Elizabeth Mitchell of Cahore, age 64

Hence George Mitchell's family tree can be refined and amended as follows:

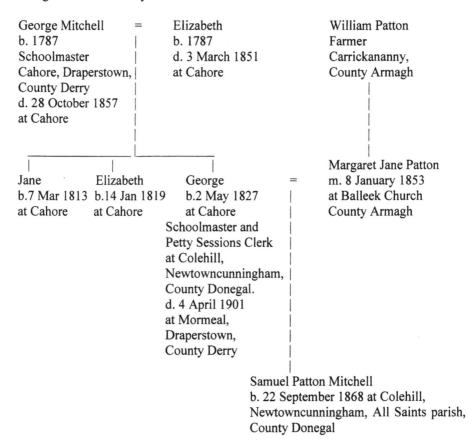

George Mitchell   =   Elizabeth   William Patton
b. 1787 | b. 1787   Farmer
Schoolmaster | d. 3 March 1851   Carrickananny,
Cahore, Draperstown, | at Cahore   County Armagh
County Derry |
d. 28 October 1857 |
at Cahore |
                       |
                       |
_____|_____ |
     | | | Margaret Jane Patton
Jane   Elizabeth   George   =   m. 8 January 1853
b.7 Mar 1813 b.14 Jan 1819 b.2 May 1827 | at Balleek Church
at Cahore   at Cahore   at Cahore | County Armagh
                            Schoolmaster and |
                            Petty Sessions Clerk |
                            at Colehill, |
                            Newtowncunningham, |
                            County Donegal. |
                            d. 4 April 1901 |
                            at Mormeal, |
                            Draperstown, |
                            County Derry |
                                             |
                            Samuel Patton Mitchell
                            b. 22 September 1868 at Colehill,
                            Newtowncunningham, All Saints parish,
                            County Donegal

GRAVESTONE INSCRIPTIONS

With civil registration of births and deaths commencing in 1864, and with the patchy survival of church records before this time, gravestone inscriptions take on a special significance. Many Church of Ireland burial registers were destroyed by fire in the Public Record Office, Dublin in 1922, while the registers of the Catholic and Presbyterian churches are especially poor regarding burial entries.

In many cases a gravestone inscription will be the only record of an ancestor's death. Yet gravestones offer much more than just the date of death; they frequently mention the townland address of the deceased together with the names, ages and dates of death of other family members. Many graves are family plots and, as a consequence, list family members and their relationship to each other.

Church of Ireland graveyards should be examined irrespective of an ancestor's religion. It was October 1829 before a Catholic cemetery opened in Dublin at Goldenbridge. Prior to the 1820s, owing to the operation of the Penal Laws, both Catholics and Protestants shared the same graveyards. Prior to the Burial Act of 1868, which permitted dissenting (i.e. Presbyterian) ministers to conduct burial services, the Church of Ireland clergy held jurisdiction over funeral services for all Protestants. Right up to the mid-19th century, it is not uncommon to find Presbyterian ministers and Methodist preachers buried in a Church of Ireland graveyard.

It is, unfortunately, true that the unkept state of many graveyards (especially those now isolated from a functioning church) and the weathering of headstones precludes the reading of many inscriptions. It is not unusual to be able to read clearly an inscription of the 18th century incised on hard Welsh slate, while those of the late 19th century, inscribed on soft limestone and sandstone headstones, have been eroded away. It must also be said that many burials in graveyards are not marked by headstones.

The gravestone located in First Garvagh Presbyterian Church, County Derry, which played its part in unravelling the McCook family story, illustrates very nicely just how much information can be gleaned from an inscription:

> In memory of Alexander McCook
> who died in the year 1872, aged 58 years
> and of his wife Jane who died in the year
> 1881, aged 66 years
> his son Archibald McCook died 19 September
> 1915, aged 77 years
> his wife Catherine died 5 December 1917 aged 72 years
> Their children
> Catherine died 18 February 1885 aged 7 years
> Graham died in infancy and their daughter
> Margaret McCullough died 4 December 1941 aged 60 years
> Hugh died 24 April 1960 aged 73 years
> Mary died 11 August 1963 aged 90 years
> Elizabeth, wife of Hugh died 1 November
> 1977 aged 79 years

From this inscription, the following family tree stretching over three generations can be drawn:

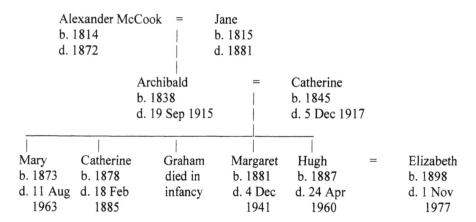

The identification of a gravestone will open many avenues for further research. Taking our example, the civil registers could be searched for the birth certificates of Archibald's children; the baptisms of Archibald and his father, Alexander, could be looked for in the baptism registers of First Garvagh Presbyterian Church, which commence in 1795; civil death registers can be searched and in the case of Alexander McCook and his wife, they would provide their exact dates of death; the 1901 and 1911 census returns should record Archibald and his family, while a will of Archibald McCook, if he made one, should be an easy matter to identify, as we know his date of death.

Clearly, on identifying an ancestor's residence, the local graveyards should be visited. The Ordnance Survey maps, at a scale of six inches to one mile, with the earliest edition dating back to the 1830s, should be consulted at a local library or online, to identify all possible graveyards.

Researchers should be aware that many old graveyards are now separated from a functioning church. With the establishment of new churches throughout the 19th century, many graveyards attached to the old church fell into disuse as new graveyards were opened beside a new church. The new church and graveyard were often located some distance away from the old church and graveyard.

You can view modern, satellite and historic maps, including 6 inch maps (1837-1842) and 25 inch maps (1888-1913), of townlands of Republic of Ireland with Ordnance Survey of Ireland Map Viewer at **map.geohive.ie/mapviewer.html**.

You can view historic maps, including first edition (1832-1846), second edition (1846-1862), third edition (1900-1907) and fourth edition (1905-1957) Ordnance Survey maps, modern maps and aerial photographs of townlands of Northern Ireland with Public Record Office of Northern Ireland's Historical Maps viewer at **www.nidirect.gov.uk/services/search-proni-historical-maps-viewer**.

A Guide to Irish Churches and Graveyards (Brian Mitchell, Genealogical Publishing Company, Baltimore, 1990) locates every church and burial ground in mid-19th-century Ireland in relation to a townland or street address. Each townland is located in its appropriate civil parish, and each parish is listed in alphabetical order in its county.

The importance of gravestone inscriptions to the genealogist can be seen in the numerous projects to transcribe them over the past hundred years.

The Journal of the Association for the Preservation of the Memorials of the Dead, in over 47 years of its existence (between 1888 and 1934), published more than 10,000 gravestone inscriptions collected from all over Ireland. Many of these journals are now online at **https://archive.org**.

Many of the county-based genealogy centers in Ireland have computerized gravestone inscriptions for their areas, and these can be searched at **www.rootsireland.ie**.

Volunteer community projects, such as Historic Graves, have transcribed over 800 graveyards in Ireland, with a concentration in counties Cork, Limerick and Tipperary, and made them available at **https://historicgraves.com**. Ireland Genealogy Projects Archives has currently indexed over 150,000 headstones, and these can be searched at **www.igp-web.com/IGPArchives**.

Transcripts of Irish Gravestone inscriptions can also be found at **www.irishgraveyards.ie**, covering mainly counties Donegal, Galway and Mayo, and **www.discovereverafter.com**, with coverage mainly in counties Armagh, Derry and Tyrone. Furthermore, Northern Irish Gravestone Inscriptions, covering the majority of graveyards in the six counties of Northern Ireland, can be searched at the website **www.ancestryireland.com/family-records/gravestone-inscriptions**.

WILLS

Wills, with their tendency to list surviving relatives – brothers, sisters, children and even grandchildren – are very important documents. It may be possible, from a will, to draw up a family tree covering up to three generations, the only limitation being the small percentage of the population – usually the better off, such as gentry, farmers and merchants – who made wills. But don't let this deter you, as a substantial proportion of the population in 19th century Ireland were tenant farmers.

Wills only take effect after the person dies and after they have been proved in court, i.e. a grant of probate has been issued. The grant of probate authenticates the will and gives the executors the power to administer the estate. Probate can take weeks, months or even years.

As well as wills you can come across "letters of administration with will annexed" and "letters of administration." A grant of letters of administration with will annexed is issued where the executors were unable to carry out the terms of the will. If a person dies without making a will, they are described as "intestate"; in this case the court can grant letters of administration (sometimes referred to as "admons"), which appoint administrators to administer the estate.

Although there is no guarantee that your ancestor made a will or, indeed, that a will has survived, as the bulk of Ireland's pre-1922 testamentary records (wills, administrations, probates, etc.) were lost in the destruction of the Public Record Office of Ireland, I would recommend a search of any indexes that exist.

Prior to 1858, ecclesiastical (consistorial) courts of the Church of Ireland, based in each diocese, were responsible for all matters of probate. Although most of these wills were destroyed in 1922 the indexes to these wills were not destroyed, and they are available in the National Archives of Ireland. There was also a central Prerogative Court, under the authority of the Archbishop of Armagh as Primate of Ireland, which dealt with testamentary matters where the deceased's property was assessed to be worth more than £5 in more than one diocese. The indexes to these Diocesan Wills and Prerogative Wills have been published in two volumes:

- *Indexes to Irish Wills, 1536-1857*, edited by William Phillimore and Gertrude Thrift, 1909-1920 (reprinted by Clearfield Company, Baltimore, 2011)
- *Index to the Prerogative Wills of Ireland, 1536-1810*, edited by Sir Arthur Vicars, 1897 (reprinted by Clearfield Company, Baltimore, 2010)

Indexes to Irish Wills is an alphabetical index of over 30,000 diocesan wills proved in the Consistorial Courts of Ireland between 1536 and 1857. Arranged by dioceses and preceded by maps showing in which dioceses the various Irish counties are situated, the indexes provide the name of the testator, his parish, county and the date of probate.

For example, this index records the following 17th-century entries in the Diocese of Derry and Raphoe for the surname Hillhouse:

Name and Residence	Date of Probate
Hillhous, Abraham, Ardikelly, parish Aghanloo	1676
Hillhous, Adam, Dunboe	1635

Hence it would appear that Abraham Hillhouse died c. 1676 in the townland of Ardikelly (spelt as Artikelly today) in the parish of Aghanloo, County Derry.

All of the Prerogative Wills of Ireland were destroyed by fire in Dublin in 1922, but before that Sir William Betham had made abstracts of the genealogical data in the wills from 1536 to 1800. In 1897 Sir Arthur Vicars prepared an index to Betham's abstracts, i.e. *Index to the Prerogative Wills of Ireland, 1536-1810*. This index has 40,000 entries arranged alphabetically by the name of the testator, showing his rank, occupation or condition; his town or county of residence; and the year when the estate was probated.

These indexes can also be searched online with the "Prerogative and diocesan copies of some wills and indexes to others, 1596–1858" database on the National Archives of Ireland Genealogy Website at **www.genealogy.nationalarchives.ie**. In Northern Ireland surviving pre-1858 will indexes found in various PRONI collections like the diocesan will and administration bond indexes can be searched using the "Name Search" database at PRONI's online archive at **www.nidirect.gov.uk/proni**.

Furthermore, you can search, by subscription at **www.findmypast.com**, the "Index of Irish Wills 1484–1858," containing over 102,000 names from surviving testamentary records, which include original documents, copies, transcripts, abstracts and extracts held in the National Archives of Ireland up to 1858. Each index entry contains the name of the person leaving a will or being covered by a grant of probate or administration. It also contains their address, sometimes their occupation, and the place where the document was proved (i.e. a diocesan court or the Prerogative court). The index also contains the names of the executors for almost half the entries, along with their addresses.

In January 1858 testamentary jurisdiction was transferred from Church control to the State. Thereafter all probates and administrations were granted at a principal registry in Dublin and eleven district registries. You could apply for a grant of probate or letters of administration at the Principal Probate Registry in all cases, but application could also be made at a District Registry within whose area the deceased had a fixed place of residence.

Unfortunately, the original wills of the Principal Registry up to 1904 and of the District Registries up to 1899 were lost in 1922 when the Public Record Office of Ireland in Dublin was destroyed. However, copies of wills that were made by the District Registries survived and these are now deposited in the National Archives of Ireland and Public Record Office of Northern Ireland. Belfast holds the will books for the districts of Belfast, Armagh and Londonderry, and Dublin has the books for the remaining eight districts. There are, unfortunately, no copies of wills proved in the principal registry in Dublin before 1922.

From 1858, summaries of every grant of probate and letters of administration were kept in printed volumes known as will calendars. An alphabetical list of names of the deceased were produced for each year recording their address and occupation, the date of death and the date of the grant of probate or letters of administration, the District Registry where the will was proved, the value of the estate, and the names of the person or persons to whom probate or administration was granted.

A complete set of these calendars for the whole of Ireland up to 1917 are held in both the National Archives of Ireland and the Public Record Office of Northern Ireland. The indexes from 1918 for the 26 counties of the Republic of Ireland and for the 6 counties of Northern Ireland are held in the National Archives of Ireland and the Public Record Office of Northern Ireland, respectively. The calendars can be a useful means to identify, relatively quickly, the date of death of an ancestor.

With the "Will Registers 1858-1900" database on the National Archives of Ireland Genealogy website at **www.genealogy.nationalarchives.ie**, you can search and view scanned images of over 550,000 records, forming the largest collection of surviving wills for the post-1858 period for the Republic of Ireland.

In Northern Ireland, will calendar entries for the District Probate Registries of Armagh, Belfast and Londonderry covering the period 1858 to 1965 can be searched using the "Will calendars" database at PRONI's online archive at **www.nidirect.gov.uk/proni**. In addition, you can then view digital images of copy wills for Armagh proved between 1858 and 1918, Belfast from 1858 to 1909 and Londonderry from 1858 to 1899.

The information you can expect to obtain from the calendar of wills and from a will itself is shown below:

CALENDAR OF WILLS 1898

| MADDEN William | 25 April. Probate of the will of William Madden late of Gartenane County Cavan Farmer who died 28 November 1897 granted at CAVAN to James Bradshaw of the Manse Irvinestown County Fermanagh Wesleyan Minister and James Graham of Bailieborough County Cavan Merchant. Effects £589 6 shillings. |

THE WILL

"I William Madden of Gartenane in the County of Cavan Farmer hereby revoke all former wills codicils and testamentary instruments heretofore made by me and declare this to be my last will and testament[.] I appoint the Reverend James Bradshaw formerly of the Manse Bailieborough in the County of Cavan and now of the Manse Irvinestown in the County of Fermanagh Wesleyan Minister and Mr James G Graham of Bailieborough in the County of Cavan Merchant to be the executors of this my will and I direct my said executors to pay my just debts and funeral and testamentary expenses[.] I confirm the gift which I have already made to my son Allen Madden of the farm upon which he now resides together with the dwelling and buildings thereon and the furniture live and dead agricultural stock crop implements of husbandry and other effects within or about or belonging to the said farm dwelling house or buildings[.] I give and bequeath to my wife Eliza Madden the sum of One Hundred pounds[.] I give and bequeath to my daughter Mary Jane Campbell the sum of forty pounds[.] I give and bequeath to my daughter Annie Eliza Anderson the sum of Forty pounds[.] I give and bequeath to my son the aforesaid Allen Madden the sum of Sixty pounds[.] I give and bequeath to my daughter Margaret Burns the sum of Sixty pounds[.] I give and bequeath to my daughter Rebecca Young now resident in Sydney the sum of Twenty pounds[.] I give and bequeath to my daughter Fanny Madden the sum of Forty pounds[.] I give and bequeath to my daughter Georgina Anderson the sum of Twenty pounds[.] I give and bequeath to my daughter Jemima Madden the sum of Twenty pounds... In witness whereof I have set my hand to this my will the 17th day of November 1897 William Madden Gartanean[.]"

You should note that the will names William's wife and his eight children and it locates the family farm in the townland of Gartenane (now spelt as Gartnaneane), Bailieborough parish, County Cavan. It gives the married names of his daughters, together with the information that one of them, Rebecca, was living in Sydney, Australia. With this information the following family tree can be drawn up:

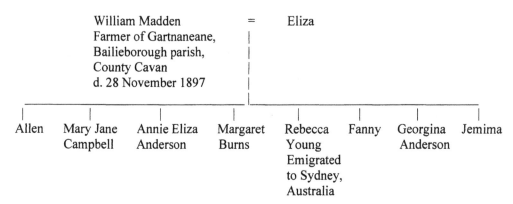

Further research can now be carried out based on information contained in this will: the 1901 census returns for Gartnaneane, County Cavan should be examined; the graveyards in the area should be checked; if the ages of William's children can be obtained from these two sources, then birth certificates or baptism entries can be searched for, depending on whether they were born before or after 1864; a death certificate, which will give William's age, could be easily obtained; the Tithe Applotment Book and Griffith's Valuation for Bailieborough parish can be searched to see if the Maddens were farming there in the early and mid-19th century, respectively, as the *Townland Index* locates Gartnaneane, the recognized spelling of the townland by the Ordnance Survey, in this parish.

1901 AND 1911 CENSUS RETURNS

Although census enumerations were carried out every decade from 1821, the earliest surviving complete return for all Ireland is that of 1901 and is complemented by that of 1911. The first four census enumerations, i.e. 1821, 1831, 1841 and 1851, were largely destroyed by fire in the Public Record Office in June 1922; and those for 1861, 1871, 1881 and 1891 were destroyed by order of government.

The 1901 and 1911 census returns record, for each member of the household, their name, age, religion, education (i.e. if they could read or write), occupation, marital status, county or city of birth, or country (if born outside Ireland), and if a speaker of Irish. The 1911 census also provides additional information on the marriage; namely the number of years married, the number of children born and the number of children still living.

The National Archives of Ireland holds the manuscript returns of the 1901 and 1911 censuses for all counties of Ireland. The Public Record Office of Northern Ireland holds microfilm copies of the census returns for the six counties of Northern Ireland.

The census enumerations of 1901 and 1911, which are arranged by townland and parish in rural areas and by street and town in urban areas, can be searched, free of charge, at **www.census.nationalarchives.ie**. All information in these census returns has been indexed and linked to digital images of the actual 1901 and 1911 census returns. This means that, in addition to being able to search the 1901 and 1911 returns by both name and place, you can view an image of the original household census form for any named individual.

As the two examples show, there is a wealth of very relevant information in the 1901 and 1911 census returns.

We can deduce from the 1901 census return that Dominick Timothy was born about 1848 and his wife, Bridget, c. 1851. There were nine children living at home with birth dates ranging from 1878 to 1894. From the birth date of the eldest son, Michael, we can assume Dominick married Bridget c. 1877. The birth certificates of the nine children could now be obtained with this information. The birth certificates will give Bridget's maiden name, and this together with a marriage date of c. 1877, deduced from the census return, should guarantee the identification of the marriage certificate of Dominick and Bridget.

As the Timothys were Catholic and as the townland of Ballincurry, where they lived, was served by the Catholic parish of Glinsk and Kilbegnet, whose registers commence in 1836, baptism entries for Dominick Timothy and his wife, Bridget, should be looked for. We are assuming here, of course, that Dominick and Bridget were born in or near Ballincurry. It is possible that the Timothys moved into the townland from another part of Galway sometime before 1901. The only clue the census gives to their birthplace is County Galway.

It is very noticeable that in the Timothy family only the mother and father could speak Irish, the children being solely English speakers. By the turn of the 20th century, the Gaelic language was generally disappearing as children began to use English at school and home.

CENSUS OF IRELAND, 1901

Townland: Ballincurry   Parish: Ballinakill   Barony: Ballymoe   County: Galway

NAME AND SURNAME		RELATION to Head of Family	RELIGIOUS PROFESSION	EDUCATION	AGE	SEX	RANK PROFESSION OR OCCUPATION	MARRIAGE	WHERE BORN	IRISH LANGUAGE
Christian	Surname									
Domnick	Timothy	Head	Roman Catholic	Read write	53	M	Herd	Married	Co Galway	Irish &
Bridget	Timothy	Wife	Roman Catholic	Read write	50	F		Married	Co Galway	English
Michael	Timothy	Son	Roman Catholic	Read write	23	M	Herd	Not married	Co Galway	
James	Timothy	Son	Roman Catholic	Read write	21	M		Not married	Co Galway	
John	Timothy	Son	Roman Catholic	Read write	19	M		Not married	Co Galway	
Domnick	Timothy	Son	Roman Catholic	Read write	17	M		Not married	Co Galway	
Mary	Timothy	Daughter	Roman Catholic	Read write	15	F		Not married	Co Galway	
Denis	Timothy	Son	Roman Catholic	Read write	13	M	Scholar	Not married	Co Galway	
Bridget	Timothy	Daughter	Roman Catholic	Read write	11	F	Scholar	Not married	Co Galway	
William	Timothy	Son	Roman Catholic	Read write	9	M	Scholar	Not married	Co Galway	
Nicholas	Timothy	Son	Roman Catholic	Read write	7	M	Scholar	Not married	Co Galway	

CENSUS OF IRELAND, 1911

Townland: Maas   Parish: Inishkeel   Barony: Boylagh   County: Donegal

NAME AND SURNAME		RELATION to Head of Family	RELIGIOUS PROFESSION	EDUCATION	AGE	RANK PROFESSION OR OCCUPATION		MARRIAGE			WHERE BORN	IRISH LANGUAGE
Christian Name	Surname							Years married	Children Born Alive	Still Living		
Patrick	Boyle	Head	Roman Catholic	Read & write	40	Farmer	Married				Co Donegal	Irish & English
Mary	Boyle	Wife	Roman Catholic	Read & write	35		Married	4	2	2	Co Donegal	English
Denis	Boyle	Son	Roman Catholic	Read & write	3		Single				Co Donegal	
Daniel	Boyle	Son	Roman Catholic	Read & write	1		Single				Co Donegal	
Hannagh	Boyle	Mother	Roman Catholic	Read & write	74	Retired Farmer	Widow				Co Donegal	Irish & English

47

The 1911 census return for the Boyle family of Maas, County Donegal identifies three generations. Again, with the information provided the relevant birth and marriage certificates should be easily obtainable. With the 1911 census you can be even more sure of the approximate marriage date.

The relevant church registers to examine would be those of Glenties Roman Catholic parish, but unfortunately baptism and marriage registers for this parish commence in 1866. This means that church registers of baptisms and marriages for the Roman Catholic population residing in the civil parish of Inishkeel don't predate civil registration (i.e. 1864).

A family tree can be constructed to highlight the information contained in this return:

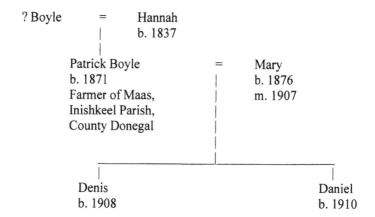

MID-19th-CENTURY GRIFFITH'S VALUATION

In Ireland the vast majority of census returns prior to 1901 no longer exist. No manuscript returns survive for 1861, 1871, 1881 and 1891 as they were destroyed by order of government during the First World War and only a few returns for 1821, 1831, 1841 and 1851 survived the Four Courts fire in 1922. Clearly this is a great loss to family historians.

It also means that sources that act as census substitutes are very important to Irish family history researchers. One such source is Griffith's Primary Valuation. Griffith's Valuation, or Primary Valuation of Ireland, was carried out between 1848 and 1864, under the direction of Sir Richard Griffith, to determine the amount of rates each household should pay towards the support of the poor within their poor law union. In detailing every head of household and occupier of land in Ireland, against a townland or street address, Griffith's Valuation is viewed as a census substitute for post-Famine Ireland. The results of the survey were published in volumes by poor law union. As the records are typewritten, except for a few parishes in the Province of Munster, there will be no problem in interpreting surnames and placenames.

This source details against every property in mid-19th-century Ireland: the occupier's name; the landlord's name; description of property; size of farm (if applicable); and rateable valuation of any buildings and land. For example, Griffith's Valuation for the poor law union of Newtownlimavady, County Derry, which was printed in 1858, records that Patrick Hassan, a tenant of Robert Ogilby, was farming 42 acres of land, in total, in the townland of Coolnamonan, Banagher parish, with a rateable valuation of £13 10 shillings:

Details of Patrick Hassan's Farm
extracted from mid-19th-century Griffith's Valuation

Townland		**COOLNAMONAN**
Parish		**BANAGHER**
Poor Law Union		**NEWTOWNLIMAVADY**
County		**LONDONDERRY**
Publication Date		**1858**
Ordnance Survey Map Numbers		30
No. and Letters of Reference to Map		9 A,B,C,D,E,F,G; 13
Occupier		**Patrick Hassan**
Immediate Lessor		Trustees Robert Ogilby
Description of Tenement		House, offices and land
Area	9A	5 A. 3 R. 20 P.
	9B	4 A 1 R. 30 P.
	9C	4 A. 1 R. 0 P.
	9D	9 A. 0 R. 30 P.
	9E	5 A. 3 R. 35 P.
	9F	7 A. 0 R. 15 P.
	9G	5 A. 3 R. 35 P.
	13d	0 A. 0 R. 30 P.
Rateable Annual Valuation of Land	9A	£4 0s. 0d.
	9B	£2 0s. 0d.
	9C	£1 16s 0d.
	9D	£3 10s. 0d.
	9E	£1 1s. 0d.
	9F	£0 5s 0d
	9G	£0 8s. 0d.
	13	£0 2s. 0d.
Rateable Annual Valuation of Buildings	13	£0 8s 0d.
Total Annual Valuation of Rateable Property		£13 10s. 0d.

Key:

Land Measurement: A. = Acres, R. = Roods, P = Perches
Money Valuation: £ = Pound, s. = shilling, d. = penny

Land Measurement: There were 40 perches to a rood and 4 roods to an acre
Money Valuation: There were 12 pennies to a shilling and 20 shillings to a pound
  Decimalisation was introduced in 1971

Total Farm Size: 42 acres 3 roods 35 perches

Note: The townland of Coolnamonan, 372 acres in size, is located in the civil parish of Banagher, County Derry and is situated five miles southwest of the town of Dungiven and one mile south of the village of Feeny.

At first glance the family historian might feel disappointed with Griffith's Valuation as it names heads of household only. With no information provided on family members within each household or relationships between householders it is not possible to confirm the nature of linkages between named people in Griffith's Valuation. It is, however, very useful in confirming the presence of a family name in a particular townland and/or parish, and in providing some insight into the frequency and distribution of surnames.

By comparing farm size, valuation of land and valuation of their home with those of their neighbors, listed in Griffith's Valuation, you can make assumptions about the economic and social standing of your ancestor.

Furthermore, a very significant feature of Griffith's Valuation was the compilation of maps to accompany the survey. Every lot number in Griffith's Valuation (recorded under the heading "No. and Letters of Reference to Map") was marked on a copy of the Ordnance Survey map (at a scale of 6 inches to 1 mile) at the Valuation Office, Dublin. This effectively means that the locations of all properties in the mid-19th century – houses and farms – can be identified once you have found your ancestor in Griffith's Valuation. In other words, with these maps you can identify with accuracy the location of the ancestral home (even if it is long gone) or farm.

The printed volumes of Griffith's Valuation and their associated valuation maps for the 26 counties of the Republic of Ireland are held in the Valuation Office, Dublin (**www.valoff.ie**) while those for the six counties of Northern Ireland are held in the Public Record Office of Northern Ireland.

Furthermore, Griffith's Valuation for all Ireland, and the associated valuation maps, are now available to search by Family Name and Place Name and view online, free of charge, at **www.askaboutireland.ie/griffith-valuation**. The Family Name Search provides transcript details, the original document page and appropriate valuation map for any selected occupier; and the Place Name Search enables you to find everyone who lived in a particular place, such as a townland, village or street in a town/city.

Griffith's Valuation also provides a window to a pattern of rural settlement, and way of life, that once dominated the Irish landscape but is now gone.

For example, an examination of Griffith's Valuation and its associated map for the townland of Coolnamonan, Banagher parish, County Derry, which was published in 1858, reveals that the families of James Hassan *(Jonny)* at 13a, James Hassan *(Tonry Due)* at 13f, Patrick Hassan at 13d, Thomas Hassan at 13e, Michael Hassan *(Jack Roe)* at 13c, Nelus Hasson at 13g, John Hassan at 13b and Michael Hassan *(Roe)* at 13h, i.e. 8 Hassan households in total, lived in a village settlement, also named as Coolnamonan. Such clusters of farm houses in "farm towns" without church, shop or public house were called clachans. I have extracted this information for the map that appears on the next page to highlight Hassan farms and their associated village home in Coolnamonan in 1858.

This source confirms a common and frustrating feature of Irish family history, namely the close association of particular parishes, and even particular townlands, with one particular surname!

HASSAN FARMS IN COOLNAMONAN
1858

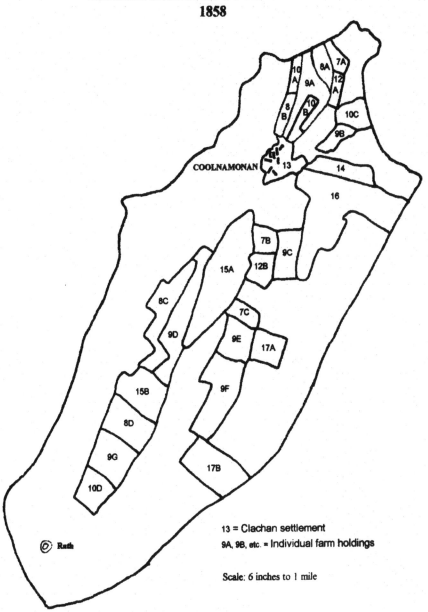

10A 8A 7A
9A 12A
8B 10B 10C
9B

COOLNAMONAN 13 14
16

7B 9C
15A 12B

8C 7C
9D 9E 17A

15B 9F

8D

9G 17B

10D

13 = Clachan settlement
9A, 9B, etc. = Individual farm holdings

Rath

Scale: 6 inches to 1 mile

Source: GRIFFITH'S VALUATION

In any townland where two or more heads of households held the same name, comments in italics were added in brackets after their names. These comments may have referred, for example, to the first name of their father, to their occupation or to a nickname associated with that particular family.

The clachan was the dominant form of rural settlement in 18th-century Ireland and it was still widespread in the 19th century in "the more harsh environments of Gaelic Ireland," i.e. in marginal areas less suited to economic farming.

Clachans were associated with a communal system of farming known as "rundale," where farms consisted of infield and outfield sections. The infield, which carried most of the crops, was divided, and subdivided among co-heirs, into unenclosed arable strips that were redistributed periodically; and the outfield, which included rough pasture and bog land, was grazed in common. Thus, the occupants of clachans were inter-related kin groups, and new houses were added to the clachan as holdings were subdivided among co-heirs.

Within these village settlements, where agriculture was subservient to the demands of cattle-herding, the bonds of kinship were close and strong. Furthermore, clachans were associated with the townland unit, the smallest and most ancient of Irish land divisions. Indeed, clachans were the nuclei of Ireland's network of townlands.

Clachans were inseparable from the rundale system of agriculture, and by the mid-19th century such village settlements had outlived their purpose and were in decay.

Although by the time of Griffith's Valuation the joint cultivation of lands had ceased in Coolnamonan, the clachan settlement had not yet been broken up into the dispersed farms that dominate the Irish landscape today. However, it is clear, from an examination of the location of farm holdings on the map, that the Hassans of Coolnamonan were farming scattered fields in and around their village settlement, i.e. the fields associated with each farm were not in one consolidated unit. This is simply a reflection of the old rundale system of agriculture whereby a tenant had his proportion in many different places. For example, in 1858 Patrick Hassan's farm (9 in the map), 42 acres in size, consisted of 7 portions (A, B, C, D, E, F and G) distributed to the north and south of his home.

The real value of Griffith's Valuation is the potential it offers to identify and map the ancestral home in sufficient detail so that you can visit that property and explore the locality for yourself and "walk in the footsteps of your ancestors."

Griffith's Valuation offers quick research results if you happen to be researching an uncommon surname. For example, an examination of this source for the surname Tethers in County Mayo, published in 1857, returns the details of two householders: John Tethers in the townland of Gorteens in Moorgagagh parish, and John Tethers in the town of Shrule in Shrule parish.

In researching the surname Eves in County Fermanagh, Griffith's Valuation, published in 1862, reveals two households of interest: John Eaves in the townland of Dooraa South in Drumkeeran parish, and Adam Eves in the town of Kesh in Magheraculmoney parish.

Griffith's Valuation will clearly be of little value, other than as an indicator of how common a surname is in any particular area, if you are researching a common name with no clues as to parish/town of origin of your ancestor.

The task of surveying and valuing properties in Ireland, i.e. Griffith's Valuation, was completed between 1848 and 1864. The valuations were then published in printed form by poor law union. Thereafter, properties were valued periodically and any changes, such as the name of a new occupier, were recorded in field notebooks, which are generally referred to as Valuation Revision Books. All changes were dated by year. Because there was always more than one year written in a book, the valuers used a different color of ink for different years.

Valuation Revision Books, held in the Valuation Office, Irish Life Centre, Abbey Street Lower, Dublin (**www.valoff.ie**), will identify and locate all occupiers of property in Republic of Ireland from mid-1850s until the early 1990s. This archive is recognized as a census substitute for the period from the 1850s to 1901 (the earliest complete census record for Ireland).

The records, which underlie and inform the printed Griffith's Valuation, i.e. Valuation Office Books covering 1824 to 1856, have been digitized by the National Archives of Ireland. These records contain over 2 million names. They provide a comprehensive assessment of the rental value of Irish lands and property from the mid-1820s to the mid-1850s and are now available online by searching "Valuation Office Books 1824-1856" on the National Archives of Ireland Genealogy website at **www.genealogy.nationalarchives.ie**.

The Valuation Revision Books for Northern Ireland are held in the Public Record Office of Northern Ireland under the reference VAL/12/B.

The Valuation Revision Books for Northern Ireland from c. 1860 to c. 1930 have been digitized, and you can search them online at **https://www.nidirect.gov.uk/information-and-services/search-archives-online/valuation-revision-books**. On entering a placename, which can be a townland, parish, street or town, the search results will return a list of revision books, in alphabetical order, by townland or street name, with dates of coverage. You then select the particular revision book or books you wish to browse through. This means that you can identify and locate all occupiers of property in Northern Ireland from mid-1850s right through to 1930. These Valuation Revision Books are not indexed by householder's name.

EARLY-19TH-CENTURY TITHE APPLOTMENT BOOKS

Again owing to the destruction of most early-19th-century census returns in Ireland, the Tithe Applotment books, like Griffith's Valuation, are records of extreme importance to family researchers.

The Tithe Applotment Books were compiled by civil parish in the period 1823 to 1837, and list tenants who paid tithe, a tax based on land valuation, paid by all, irrespective of religious denomination, for the support of the Established Church (i.e. Church of Ireland). The year of tithe assessment varied from parish to parish. The tithe books only name heads of rural households. They give no details on family members, as they merely list heads of household, together with size and valuation of their farm and townland address.

For example, the tithe book for Ardstraw parish, County Tyrone, which was surveyed in 1834, identifies Samuel Craig farming 50 acres in the townland of Glenglush and assessed to pay tithe of £1 0 shillings and 10 pennies:

Details of Samuel Craig's Farm
extracted from early-19th-century Tithe Applotment Book

Townland	**GLENGLUSH**
Parish	**ARDSTRAW**
Diocese	**DERRY**
County	**TYRONE**
Year of Assessment	**1834**
Landholder's Name	**Samuel Craig**
Amount of Acres per statute measure	50 acres 0 roods 34 perches
First Quality	10 acres 0 roods 0 perches
Second Quality	20 acres 0 roods 0 perches
Third Quality	20 acres 0 roods 34 perches
Acreable Rate 1st Quality	14 shillings
Acreable Rate 2nd Quality	7 shillings
Acreable Rate 3rd Quality	2 shillings
Annual Value	£16 - 0 shillings - 5 pennies
Amount of Composition	£1 - 0 shillings - 10 pennies

Key:

Land Measurement in acres, roods and perches
Money Valuation in Pounds (£), shillings (s) and pennies (d)

Land Measurement: There were 40 perches to a rood and 4 roods to an acre
Money Valuation: There were 12 pennies to a shilling and 20 shillings to a pound
Decimalisation was introduced in 1971

Note: The townland of Glenglush, 373 acres in size, is located in the civil parish of Ardstraw, County Tyrone and is situated 7 miles southwest of the town of Strabane and 5 miles northwest of the town of Newtownstewart.

This source usually details against every landholder in early-19th-century Ireland: the landholder's name; size of farm (in acres, roods and perches); quality of land (1st class, 2nd, 3rd etc.); valuation of land; and amount of tithe composition (in pounds [£], shillings [s], and pennies [d]).

At first glance the family historian might feel disappointed with tithe books as they name heads of household only. With no information provided on family members within each household or relationships between householders it is not possible to confirm the nature of linkages between named people in tithe books. Tithe books, furthermore, record the names of tenant farmers but not of urban dwellers or landless labourers. A landholder may also appear more than once on a list, thereby indicating that they held more than one piece of land. However, as tithe books exist for most parishes in Ireland, and as they detail every occupier of land in Ireland against a townland address, they are viewed as a census substitute for pre-Famine rural Ireland. The tithe books, in many instances, will be the last official record of many who emigrated from Ireland during and after the Famine of 1845-1849.

Published in volumes, by parish, tithe books for Northern Ireland can be examined at the Public Record Office of Northern Ireland and for the Republic of Ireland in the National Archives of Ireland.

Tithe books for the Republic of Ireland have been digitized and can be searched and viewed online, free of charge, at **www.titheapplotmentbooks.nationalarchives.ie**. As well as being able to browse the tithe books, by selecting county, parish and townland you can also search the database by householder's name.

Tithe books for Northern Ireland have also been digitized and they can be viewed, free of charge, by searching PRONI's e-catalogue at **www.nidirect.gov.uk/services/search-pronis-ecatalogue**; select the "Browse" button and enter FIN/5/A in the search box. The Tithe books are catalogued alphabetically by parish name, and they can be searched at townland level within each parish by selecting the appropriate digital view. They are not indexed by householder's name.

A name index, however, to some 200,000 landholders extracted from the tithe books of 233 parishes in the six counties of Northern Ireland – Armagh, Antrim, Down, Fermanagh, Londonderry, and Tyrone – can be viewed, free of charge, on registration, by searching the Census Substitutes database at **www.rootsireland.ie**.

In tithe books, as in Griffith's Valuation, land was measured in acres, roods and perches. As a generalization, there were 40 perches to a rood and 4 roods to an acre.

Different land measurements have been used in Irish land surveys since the 17th century. In tithe books land was often measured in Irish Plantation acres, and in the mid-19th-century Griffith's Valuation in English acres or Statute acres. The "Irish" or "plantation" acre was equal to 1.62 "statute" or "English" acres. An "Irish" acre is, therefore, bigger than an "English" acre. Thus, 5 "Irish" acres were equivalent to 8 "English" or "Statute" acres. In Ulster, in particular, land could also be measured in "Scottish" acres. The "Cunningham" or "Scottish" acre was equal to 1.29 "Statute" acres. Thus, 5 "Irish" acres are equivalent to 6.45 "Scottish" acres. Researchers, therefore, need to be aware of these differences when comparing farm sizes in different surveys.

The main, if not sole, reason for using the tithe books is to identify the townland address of an ancestor. Knowledge of a townland address gives access to many other record sources.

For example, the tithe book for Killardry parish, then better known as Killaldriffe parish, County Tipperary identifies Thomas Dwyer farming 20 acres and paying tithe of £1 10 pennies in the townland of Ballydrehid. This means that the local Catholic parish registers, namely Bansha and Kilmoyler, which date back to 1820, could be searched for Dwyer entries. The local graveyards should be visited; the Ordnance Survey sheet number 75, which maps Ballydrehid townland at six inches to one mile, should be consulted to identify them.

The tithe book for Killardry parish was compiled in 1834, so Griffith's Valuation for the same parish, which was published in 1851, should be checked to see if the Dwyers continued to live in Ballydrehid. Griffith's Valuation, in fact, identifies four Dwyer households living in the townland: Michael farming 10 acres, James 14 acres, Jeremiah 3 acres, and Julia 24 acres. This illustrates the major limitation of the tithe books and Griffith's Valuation, namely the lack of sufficient information to confirm family connections. We will need to rely on church registers to make the link between the Thomas Dwyer identified in 1834 tithe book and the four Dwyer households farming and living in Ballydrehid in 1851 Griffith's Valuation.

The 1901 and 1911 census returns can also be checked for Dwyer households still residing at Ballydrehid at the turn of the 20th century. A search of 1901 and 1911 census returns reveal that one Dwyer family was living there; namely the family of Thomas and Honoria O'Dwyer.

As the tithe books were handwritten and compiled before standards in the spelling of both surnames and place names became established, care should be taken in researching them. For example, the townland known today as Tonaghbane in Kildrumsherdan parish, County Cavan appears as thus in Griffith's Valuation, but was spelled in the tithe book as both Tonaghbawn and Tunnaghbaun.

In researching the McKay family of Drumard townland, Tamlaght O'Crilly parish, County Derry, I noted three different spellings of the name in three different records! It was McCoy in the 1831 census, McCay in the tithe book of 1833 and McKay in Griffith's Valuation of 1859.

With the seven record sources detailed in this chapter, you should be able to construct a family tree on most family lines going back six or seven generations. Each of the records will supply a wealth of relevant information on their own account. But equally important, each of these sources, and the information they contain, hold clues to aid the identification of other sources. By this process of one line of research leading to another, a family tree will spring to life.

Don't despair if you find that the church register you require was destroyed or starts too late. Obstacles are there to be surmounted; if one avenue shuts its doors to you, look for another. You might identify a gravestone listing three generations of your ancestors. Initially you might be disappointed that your ancestor was born in 1863, thus missing out on civil registration, but their later identification in a baptism register will more than compensate for it. In fact, there is nothing quite like the excitement of identifying an ancestor you, at one time, thought was lost to you.

OTHER RECORD SOURCES

The seven record sources described in the previous chapter will be the starting points for those researching their family tree. The sources described in this section are very valuable to the family researcher, but I would advise turning to them only after exhausting the seven major sources. The major records, in all cases, will be more comprehensive in terms of family detail provided and in terms of their coverage of Ireland.

The early census returns of 1821, 1831, 1841 and 1851 would be classified as major record sources if they had survived for much greater areas of Ireland. Census substitutes, such as the Hearth Money Rolls of the 1660s and the Flax Growers' Lists of 1796, don't list all heads of household. Although records in the Registry of Deeds date back to 1708, there is no guarantee an ancestor would have registered their property transactions. Records of great genealogical value may be found among the business records of the large landed estates, but again there is no certainty.

19TH-CENTURY CENSUS RETURNS

Although census enumerations were carried out every decade in Ireland from 1821, the earliest surviving complete return for all Ireland is that of 1901. The first four census enumerations, i.e. 1821, 1831, 1841 and 1851, were largely destroyed by fire in the Public Record Office at the Four Courts, Dublin in June 1922; and those for 1861, 1871, 1881 and 1891 were destroyed by order of government.

The example of one such return from the 1821 census for Inisheer Island, County Galway, shows what a serious loss this is to the genealogist. With this return it is possible to calculate the approximate dates of birth for all members of the family and deduce the marriage date of the parents. It can be assumed that Pat Faherty married Bridget around 1811, as their first-born son was aged 9 in 1821. (Never, though, rely on alleged ages of adults as being accurate, use them only as a guide!) The observation column provides very interesting information as to how the occupants of one of the Arran Islands earned their living – "by fishing and kelp making."

Any surviving fragments from the census returns of 1821 to 1851 are held in the National Archives of Ireland with microfilm copies in the Public Record Office of Northern Ireland. Surviving census fragments for 1821, 1831, 1841 and 1851 can be searched online at **www.census.nationalarchives.ie**.

The loss of census returns for many areas has meant that records such as the early-19th-century tithe books and mid-19th-century Griffith's Valuation, which survive for all Ireland, have taken on added importance.

Owing to the survival of an abstract of the 1831 census for County Derry, it means that the early-19th-century tithe books are less relevant as a source for the family historian in this county than in the other counties of Ireland.

The 1831 census return for County Derry, arranged by parish and townland, lists: the name of each head of household; the number of individual families in each house; the number of males and females, including servants, in each household; and their religious denomination. Although this source lists the names of all heads of households in County Derry, 40,000 in total, it doesn't name the other family members within each household.

CENSUS OF IRELAND, 1821

Townland: Inisheer   Parish: Arran   Barony: Arran   County: Galway

No of House	No of Stories	NAMES OF INHABITANTS	AGE	OCCUPATION	No of Acres	OBSERVATIONS
1	1	Pat Faherty	40	Farmer & Fisherman	Cartron ¼	The inhabitants of this Island live by fishing and kelp making they take large quantities of Cod Ling Haddock Glassin and Herrings from Christmas to the Middle of April when they commence kelp making which they continue to the end of September the best kelp at the Galway Market is here manufactured
		Bridget Faherty his wife	30			
		Margaret Faherty Daughter	9			The land here and in all the Islands of Arran is never in any instance let by the acre it is set by the parcell Denominated Quarters Half Quarters Cartrons Half Cartrons fourths of Cartrons Eights of Cartrons and Sixteenths of Cartrons
		John Faherty Son	6			
		Peter Faherty Son	3			
		Kate Faherty Daughter	1			
		Ned Tolan	18	House Servant		
		Anthony Joyce	35	A Schoolmaster unemployed		The Tillage is mostly potatoes with very little Rye in this Island.

58

Pension search summaries act as a partial reconstruction of the 1841 and 1851 census returns. The Old Age Pension Act was introduced in 1908. For persons applying to the local Pensions Officer for a pension with no proof of age (i.e. that they were 70 years old), searches were requested of the 1841 and 1851 census returns at the Public Record Office, Dublin. These searches were all completed before the fire in the Public Record Office in 1922.

The Old Age Pension search summaries for the Republic of Ireland are held in the National Archives of Ireland; those for Northern Ireland are in the Public Record Office of Northern Ireland. Pension search summaries for the Republic of Ireland can be examined online at the National Archives Genealogy Website at **www.genealogy.nationalarchives.ie** by selecting Census Search Forms, 1841-51. Pension search summaries for the nine counties of Ulster were published in two books by Josephine Masterson: *Ireland: 1841/1851 Census Abstracts (Republic of Ireland)* and *Ireland: 1841/1851 Census Abstracts (Northern Ireland)* (Genealogical Publishing Company, Baltimore, 1999).

NEWSPAPERS

Birth notices, marriage announcements, and obituaries contained within the pages of newspapers can provide very useful information, especially when it is remembered that many towns in Ireland had their own paper. In Dublin by the mid-1750s *Faulkner's Dublin Journal*, *Freeman's Journal*, *Dublin Hibernian Journal* and *Dublin Evening Post* were beginning to carry regular and fairly numerous marriage and obituary notices for the city and county of Dublin. Many provincial towns also had newspapers dating back to the 18th century, such as *Belfast Newsletter* from 1737, *Cork Journal* from 1753, *Limerick Chronicle* from 1768 and *Londonderry Journal* from 1772.

The problem with newspapers, and searching through them, is that because of the frequency of their publication, it is very crucial to be able to narrow down the field of search to a fairly precise date. The time spent looking up newspapers, however, is well justified, especially if it comes up with an obituary, as they can provide a quite detailed life history. For example, the obituary of Thomas Gordon, who died 8 February 1911 at The Diamond, Derry, aged 91, was published in the *Londonderry Sentinel* of Thursday 9 February 1911:

"Of an old Scottish stock, the great-grandfather of the deceased came from Aberdeen and settled in county Fermanagh. Mr. Gordon was born at Churchill. He served his apprenticeship in Enniskillen, and afterwards was in employment in Cavan in the establishment owned by Mr. Matthew Lough….In 1847 he started business in Coleraine, and in 1861 he transferred to Londonderry. He was, therefore, a citizen of fifty years standing. His entire business life in Londonderry was passed in the one building, the well-known shop and residence in The Diamond….In 1849 Mr. Gordon married Harriet Remington, the daughter of an Irish Wesleyan missionary to Newfoundland."

This obituary suggests that the 17th-century origins of the Gordon family will be found in Scotland in the vicinity of Aberdeen.

The historic content of a wide range of Irish provincial newspapers can be searched at the British Newspaper Archive at **www.britishnewspaperarchive.co.uk** and Irish Newspaper Archives at **www.irishnewsarchive.com**. For example, Irish Newspaper Archives has indexed and digitized the *Belfast Newsletter* from 1738, while the British Newspaper Archive has indexed and digitized the content of the three newspapers that served 19th-century Derry city:

Derry Journal 1825-1955, *Londonderry Sentinel* 1829-1959, and *Londonderry Standard* 1836-1872.

DIRECTORIES

These are a useful source of information for people living in the towns of Ireland. The directories were usually organized by trade, such as grocers, bankers, publicans, coopers, ship builders, tanners, rope makers and brewers, to name but a few. Under each trade were listed the people carrying out that trade, together with their address. The local gentry, clergy and professional people were also noted.

The first trade directory for Dublin city appeared in 1751, and by 1799 the list of merchants within its pages exceeded 4,300. The first provincial town to issue a directory was Limerick in 1769, to be followed by Cork in 1787. In 1820 J. Pigot & Co. issued the *Commercial Directory of Ireland*, covering the main towns. Further editions appeared in 1824, 1846, 1856, 1870, 1881 and 1894. The National Archives, Dublin and the Public Record Office of Northern Ireland, Belfast and the National Library of Ireland hold the greatest number of directories, but local libraries will hold directories for their local area.

Directories for many town in Ulster covering the years 1819 to 1900 can be searched at the Public Record Office of Northern Ireland's online archive, which can be found at **www.nidirect.gov.uk/information-and-services/search-archives-online/street-directories**.

From the second half of the 19th century, some towns also published street directories. For example, the 'First Annual Issue' of the *Derry Almanac and Directory* was published by the *Londonderry Sentinel* in 1861. The early issues contained a "Professional Directory" and "Trades Directory" for Derry city and for nearby towns and villages in Counties Derry, Donegal and Tyrone.

From 1868 right through to 1949, inclusive, each annual edition of the *Derry Almanac* also contained a "Street Directory" where all heads of households were identified against their street address in Derry city. Each "Street Directory" was printed in alphabetical order by street name; they were not indexed by householder's name. The recording of house numbers, against each householder, first appeared in the *Almanac* of 1897. It should be said that changes in local numbering of streets can present pitfalls to researchers using street directories and other historic documents.

SCHOOL REGISTERS

The widespread and comprehensive keeping of school registers had to await the introduction of the national system of schooling in 1832 and, in particular, the 1860s, when many registers start. Prior to 1832, schooling depended on support from churches, charitable endowments and private funding. The second report of the Commissioners of Irish Education Inquiry of 1826-27 does list all schools, on a parish basis, together with the number and religion of their pupils. It furthermore names all teachers. Few registers, however, survive for these schools.

The national schoolhouse became a feature of the Irish countryside in the second half of the 19th century and the school registers they kept can be of great value to the genealogist. To identify the appropriate register, you need to know at least the parish your ancestor lived in, as in the nine counties of Ulster alone 2,500 national schools were established between 1832 and

1860. The information provided of name, date of birth and religion of pupil, together with the father's occupation and address, should be sufficient to enable the identification of an ancestor, even in those areas where your surname is common. The National Archives, Dublin and the Public Record Office of Northern Ireland hold many school registers.

17TH- AND 18TH- CENTURY CENSUS SUBSTITUTES

Flax Growers' Lists

In 1796 lists were compiled by county and parish of farmers who were entitled to a grant for sowing flax seed. The grant was to be in the form of equipment used in the linen industry.

In the 18th and 19th centuries, flax was one of Ireland's chief crops. Although linen production accounted for almost half of Ireland's exports, it was very much a cottage industry. Flax was grown on very small farms, prepared and spun into linen yarn and woven into webs of cloth by families in their own homes, and sold in linen markets in towns to the linen drapers and bleachers who finished the linens for sale or export.

However, as people were more interested in spinning and weaving than cultivation, the Irish Linen Board came up with a plan in 1796 to encourage farmers to grow more flax seed. Free spinning wheels or looms were to be granted to farmers who planted a certain acreage of their holding with flax. A quarter-acre of flax equaled one spinning wheel and those who grew over five acres or more received a loom. County inspectors were appointed to receive claims from the growers, and county lists, detailing the civil parish of residence (but not the townland address), were published as official documents of the Board.

The names of over 56,000 recipients of these awards have survived in printed form arranged by county and parish. The economy of Ulster, in particular, was tied to linen production. The northern counties of Tyrone and Donegal had the largest number of spinning wheels awarded. Ulster had 65% of the wheels, the remaining were distributed throughout Ireland with no records existing for Dublin and Wexford.

The only known surviving copy of the records is held at the Linen Hall Library of Belfast (**https://linenhall.com**). Public Record Office of Northern Ireland holds a photocopy of the original volume. An online version of the Flax Growers' List is free to search, either by county or by surname, at **www.failteromhat.com/flax1796.php**.

The Religious Census of 1766

In March 1766 the Irish Parliament authorized an all-Ireland religious census. Church of Ireland (Protestant) clergy in each parish were instructed to return a list of the families in their parishes, identifying whether they were Protestant or Catholic.

Unfortunately, none of the 1766 returns list all members of a household. An examination of the returns shows great variations in their usefulness. For example, the return for Cumber parish, County Derry merely gives a numerical breakdown of Protestants and Catholics in each of its constituent townlands. It, therefore, serves no purpose for the genealogist. The returns for Nantinan parish, County Limerick names all Protestant householders but doesn't provide their townland address, while that for Artrea parish, County Tyrone lists against each townland the occupiers and their religion.

Most of the original returns were lost in the fire at the Public Record Office in 1922. However, transcripts do survive for many parishes, especially in counties Cork, Limerick, Londonderry, Louth, Tipperary, Tyrone and Wicklow. The National Archives of Ireland has compiled a table that shows where to find surviving returns for the whole of Ireland; it can be viewed at **www.nationalarchives.ie/PDF/ReligiousCensus.pdf**.

Ancestry.com has indexed about 11,000 names taken from transcripts of 1766 census returns created by Tenison Groves. Nearly all the records relate to parishioners in Northern Ireland.

Groves Manuscripts, at reference T808 in the Public Record Office of Northern Ireland, contains, in 27 boxes, around 20,000 copies of genealogical working papers, comprising testamentary papers, notes, abstracts, census substitutes including freeholder lists, Hearth Money Rolls, poll books, 1766 religious census and other material, dating from c. 1650-1900. It was compiled and copied by Tenison Groves, a professional genealogist and antiquarian who worked at the Public Record Office of Ireland in Dublin from around 1900 until after the Four Courts Fire of 1922. The great importance of this archive is that it contains extracts from documents which were destroyed in the Irish Civil War in 1922.

A partial index to 1766 census returns can also be searched at Public Record Office of Northern Ireland's online archive at **www.nidirect.gov.uk/information-and-services/search-archives-online/name-search**.

Protestant Householders' Lists of 1740

In 1740 lists of Protestant heads of household were compiled – by county, barony and parish – by collectors of the Hearth Tax. The originals were destroyed in 1922 but transcripts survive for parts of the survey in Counties Armagh, Antrim, Derry, Donegal, Down, Longford and Tyrone. For example, this source survives for all County Derry parishes and names 8,646 Protestant residents; in some cases only their parish address is provided, while in others the townland address is given. Copies of these lists are held by the Public Record Office of Northern Ireland and by the National Library of Ireland in Dublin.

This source will identify many British "planters" who settled in Ulster in large numbers at the end of the 17th century. It is estimated, in the 15 years after 1690 and the Glorious Revolution, that 50,000 people came to Ulster from Scotland. It is further estimated that by 1715, when Scottish migration to Ulster had virtually ceased, the Presbyterian population of Ulster, i.e. of essentially Scottish origin, stood at 200,000.

A partial index to 1740 Protestant Householders can be searched at the websites **www.nidirect.gov.uk/information-and-services/search-archives-online/name-search** and at **www.ancestryireland.com/scotsinulster**.

Hearth Money Rolls

The first Hearth Money act was passed in the Irish Parliament in 1662 as a means to increase government revenue. A tax of two shillings was to be raised for every hearth or "other place used for firing." A list was then kept by county, giving the name and amount each householder had to pay under their townland address. Copies of the hearth lists subsequently drawn up between 1663 and 1666 exist in full for the Ulster counties of Antrim, Armagh, Donegal,

Fermanagh, Londonderry, Monaghan, and Tyrone and for Counties Dublin, Kilkenny, Louth, Sligo, Tipperary, Westmeath and Wicklow. Extracts, however, do survive for other counties. Surviving hearth money rolls will be found in the National Archives, Dublin and Public Record Office of Northern Ireland.

At **www.ancestryireland.com/scotsinulster** you can search, by surname, the Hearth Money Rolls of the 1660s for counties in Ulster.

Muster Rolls

Throughout the 17th century, landlords mustered their tenants periodically to identify adult males capable of military service. Most of the names in these rolls are of Planter or British origin, although a few native Irish names are also recorded. The Muster Roll of 1630 is by far the most extensive. For example, this muster names 1,931 men who resided on 19 estates in County Derry and 1,269 men who resided on 20 estates in County Donegal.

Men and Arms: The Ulster Settlers, c. 1630, by R. J. Hunter (Ulster Historical Foundation, Belfast, 2012), records the names of 13,147 adult males, listed under the names of their landlord, who were mustered in the nine counties of Ulster in c. 1630. Most of the men who mustered were English and Scottish settlers and, in the absence of comprehensive parish and estate records, muster rolls are the nearest one has to a census of the British population of early-17th-century Ulster.

On 22 October 1641 the native Irish, under Sir Phelim O'Neill, rose in rebellion in Counties Derry and Tyrone, and the walled city of Derry became a refuge for Protestant settlers. The "Muster rolls of foot companies in the garrison of Londonderry," dated May 1642-August 1643 names 905 men, organized in nine foot companies, consisting of 90 officers and 815 soldiers, who defended Derry's walls during the Irish Rebellion of 1641 and the threatened siege of the city during the winter of 1641/42.

Defenders of The Plantation of Ulster 1641-1691, by Brian Mitchell (Clearfield, Baltimore, 2010), names the 905 men who defended the walls of Derry during the Irish Rebellion of 1641 and a further 1,660 "defenders" who were named in contemporary sources as playing an active or supportive role in the Williamite War in Ireland, 1689-1691, which included the 1689 Siege of Derry.

PLANTATION AND SETTLEMENT RECORDS

Various 17th-century surveys record the changes in ownership and occupation resulting from the land confiscations of that period.

The extensive changes in landownership following the Cromwellian settlement are recorded in the Civil Survey and Down Survey, both begun in 1654. Confiscated lands were identified, surveyed and mapped to record land ownership, land boundaries, and land use, whether wood, bog, mountain, arable, meadow or pasture.

The Civil Survey of 1654–56 of landholding in Ireland was carried out by an inquisition that visited each barony and took depositions from landholders based on parish and townland, with written descriptions of their boundaries. The Survey covered 27 of Ireland's 32 counties, but excluded the five counties in Connacht.

The original Civil Survey records were destroyed by fire in 1711, but a complete set of copies for ten counties – Derry, Donegal, Dublin, Kildare, Limerick, Meath, Tipperary, Tyrone, Waterford and Wexford – and partial copies for Cork, Kerry and Kilkenny were discovered in the 19th century. The Survey was published by the Irish Manuscripts Commission in the early 20th century, and digital copies are available on its website, which can be accessed at **www.irishmanuscripts.ie/servlet/Controller?action=digitisation_backlist**.

The Civil Survey was separate from the Down Survey, a cartographic survey, which began while the Civil Survey was in progress, and made use of Civil Survey data to guide its progress. The Down Survey of 1656-58 maps out in great detail the dramatic transfer in land ownership from Catholics to Protestants in 17th-century Ireland, and it can be examined at **http://downsurvey.tcd.ie/down-survey-maps.php**. All counties except Galway, Roscommon and Mayo were mapped in the Down Survey.

The Books of Survey and Distribution were compiled between the 1650s and 1680s owing to the need to establish land ownership following the restoration of Charles II in 1660 and further forfeitures resulting from an Act of 1688. The Books of Survey and Distribution, as the example from County Clare shows, can record up to three different landowners for any given area through the 17th century:

Parish: Digart   Barony: Inchiquin   County: Clare

Column 1	2	3	4	5	6	7	8	9
101	Teige O'Bryan	Carrowmenough Arable & Pasture	73	73	Lord Clare	73	Francis Burton	Θ

EXPLANATION OF THE BOOKS OF SURVEY AND DISTRIBUTION

Column 1	Reference number in the Down Survey Parish map.
Column 2	Proprietor in 1640/41.
Column 3	Name of Townland and description of the land.
Column 4	Number of acres of cultivable land.
Column 5	Number of acres redistributed after the Cromwellian settlement.
Column 6	Name of proprietor established by Charles II.
Column 7	Number of acres purchased after the forfeiture of 1688.
Column 8	Name of the purchaser of the land forfeited after 1688. If Column 8 is blank, it indicates that the landowner who acquired the land under Charles II continued to retain it in 1703.
Column 9	The Θ symbol after the purchaser's name in Column 8 indicates that he was a purchaser of a forfeited estate of 1688, at the Trustee's sale, 1701-1703.

The Books of Survey and Distribution, laid out in tabular form on a barony and parish basis, survive for all counties except Dublin, Louth and Meath. A set of the Books of Survey and Distribution can be found in the Annesley Papers, at reference D1854/1, in Public Record Office of Northern Ireland. The Books for Clare, Galway, Mayo and Roscommon have been published by the Irish Manuscripts Commission, with digital copies that you can view at **www.irishmanuscripts.ie/servlet/Controller?action=digitisation_backlist**.

MILITARY RECORDS

Some of the Penal Laws against Catholics were reversed with the Catholic Relief Act of 1778, which allowed Catholics to join the British Army and purchase property if they took an oath of allegiance.

At this time, the British Army needed soldiers to fight in the American Revolutionary War (1775-1783, also known as American War of Independence). Many Irish Catholics from this point on would see the army as an opportunity for employment to support their families. It has been estimated that during the American War of Independence, 16% of the rank and file and 31% of the Officers in the British Army were Irishmen.

Irishmen, Catholic and Protestant, joined the British Army and the Royal Navy during the Napoleonic Wars (1803-1815). The Irish would swell the ranks to the extent that by 1813 the British Army's total manpower was "1/2 English, 1/6 Scottish and 1/3 Irish." At the Battle of Trafalgar in 1805, around a quarter of the Royal Navy crew present were Irishmen.

Many Irishmen and members of the Irish diaspora in Britain served in both World War I (1914-1918) and World War II (1939-1945) as part of the British forces. Over 200,000 men from Ireland fought in World War I; it is estimated that about 30,000 died serving in Irish regiments of the British forces, and about 49,600 died altogether.

Details of soldiers' service may be held in Service Records, Medal Records and Unit War Diaries. British military records predating 1920 are held in the National Archives, Kew, London (**www.nationalarchives.gov.uk**) and those after 1920 by the Ministry of Defence (**www.gov.uk/government/collections/requests-for-personal-data-and-service-records**).

The Military Records collection at **www.ancestry.com** contains a comprehensive range of British military records, war records and service records dating from the early 1700s.

This collection of British military records includes three databases of great interest to those with ancestors who served in the British Army in the 18th and 19th centuries, namely:

- Ireland, Royal Hospital Kilmainham Pensioner Discharge Documents, 1724-1924

Pensions for soldiers discharged from Irish regiments in the British Army were administered by the Royal Hospital Kilmainham near Dublin. The Royal Hospital Kilmainham dates back to 1680 and provided a home for retired soldiers. While some pensioners surrendered their pension to the hospital and lived there ("in-pensioners"), many more lived outside the hospital and received their pensions elsewhere ("out-pensioners"). Pensions from the Royal Hospital Kilmainham were administered to soldiers who had served for at least 12 years in the British Army. This collection consists of discharge documents for pensioners who served between 1724 and 1924. For each record, details may include a brief description of the pensioner together with age, place of birth, particulars of service and the reason for discharge.

- UK, Royal Hospital Chelsea Pensioner Admissions and Discharges, 1715-1925

Most pensions for non-Irish regiments were administered by the Royal Hospital Chelsea in London. The Royal Hospital Chelsea was the administrative office for the British Army and was responsible for distributing pension payments to British soldiers since the 1680s. This collection is made up of registers of the award of out-pensions of the Royal Hospital Chelsea to soldiers discharged from the British Army who had served for at least 12 years between 1715 and 1925. For each record, details may include a brief description of the pensioner together with age, place of birth, particulars of service and the reason for discharge.

- UK, Royal Hospital Chelsea Pensioner Soldier Service Records, 1760-1920

This collection comprises service documents of soldiers (but not officers) who either became in-pensioners or out-pensioners of the Royal Hospital Chelsea between 1760 and 1920. By 1815 there were already 36,757 out-pensioners and they remained under military discipline to some extent; they formed a reserve pool to be called on in case of wartime emergency or domestic crisis.

Databases of particular interest, in the Military Records collection at **www.ancestry.com**, to those researching ancestors who served in the British Army during World War I include:

- Ireland, Casualties of World War I, 1914-1922

This data collection contains the book *Ireland's Memorial Records* – an eight-volume set compiled by The Committee of the Irish National War Memorial, originally published in 1923, which names 49,647 Irish men and women who died in World War I.

A search of "Ireland's Memorial Records 1914-1918" for George Mitchell, son of the Reverend Robert James and Ann Mitchell of Trillick, County Tyrone, returns:

MITCHELL, G. Rank, 2nd Lieutenant, attached 45th Sikhs, Indian Army; killed in action, February 1, 1917; born Ireland

- British Army WWI Medal Rolls Index Cards, 1914-1920

This collection, containing 4.8 million people, is the most complete listing of individuals who fought in British Army in World War I. The Index Cards compiled by the Army Medal Office were created in order to keep in one place details about a soldier's medal entitlement.

- British Army WWI Service Records, 1914-1920

This data collection contains 3.6 million British Army service records. World War II bombing raid on the War Office in London destroyed about 60% of 6.5 million British Army World War I service records.

- British Army WWI Pension Records, 1914-1920

This database contains 2.1 million British Army pension records.

Once the regiment in which your ancestor served is known, then you can make a search for publications and/or make contact with the Regimental Museum to identify Unit War Diaries, which will detail campaigns fought, with daily reports of unit activity. With such War Diaries, you can build up a mental picture of your ancestor's tour of duty.

In our example, George Mitchell was a second lieutenant with an Indian Army regiment, the 45th Sikhs. In 2013 Naval & Military Press, in association with the Imperial War Museum, published *Regimental History of the 45th Rattray's Sikhs during the Great War and after, 1914-1921* by Lieutenant-Colonel R. H. Anderson. This book is, in effect, a War Diary for 45th Sikhs, with daily reports of operations in the period 1914 to 1921. In summary, the Regiment spent the period 1914-1916 on India's North-West frontier, 1916-1918 fighting the Turkish army in Mesopotamia (then a Turkish possession in present-day Iraq) and 1919-1921 in Kurdistan.

George Mitchell was killed in action on 1 February 1917 "at relief of Kut." The old town of Kut in eastern Iraq was located within a sharp "U" bend of the Tigris River, some 100 miles southeast of Baghdad, 100 miles northwest of Amarah and 200 miles northwest of Basra.

The regimental history of the 45th Sikhs throws light on a lesser-known battlefield of World War I, namely the advance into Iraq by an Anglo-Indian army in Spring of 1917 and, in particular, the brutal Trench warfare of January/February 1917 in British attempts to relieve Kut.

Orders for further assault on Kut, to be delivered by the 45th Sikhs and 36th Sikhs, were issued at 5.45 p.m. on 31 January [1917].

"The morning [of 1 February] broke very misty, but cleared into a gloriously fine day, so much so that about 11 a.m. Kut stood out very clearly and the inhabitants could be plainly seen sitting on the roofs of the houses watching the events on the plain on which we were operating.

"The 45th under the command of Lieutenant-Colonel H. B. Rattray D.S.O. (strength: 8 British Officers, 17 Indian Officers, and 562 Other Ranks) advanced to the attack at 12.10 p.m. on a frontage of 260 yards, under cover of a terrific artillery bombardment, with their right [flank] on the River Hai, and the 36th Sikhs on their left." They advanced in eight lines of double platoons at 50 yards distance and "as the Regiment went over, they shook out into perfect lines at once, and moved forward as steadily as if on an ordinary parade.

"The last four waves, 'B' and 'A' Companies, suffered considerably from the machine gun fire that enfiladed the 36th Sikhs on our left, whilst they were crossing the ground between Mathews' and Gunning Trenches. They pressed on, however, to the 'Bank.' Second Lieutenant G Mitchell, 'A' Company, was killed whilst crossing 'No man's land.' At this period the fighting was all hand-to-hand, and the Turkish counter-attacks began to come down the flanks of both lines of trenches."

Of the 587 men of the 45th Sikhs who advanced on the morning of 1 February 1917 against Turkish frontline trenches, only 105 men returned unscathed, three hours later, when the orders were given to retire from the battlefield. Kut was eventually recaptured on 23 February 1917.

The website of the Commonwealth War Graves Commission, **www.cwgc.org**, honors the 1.7 million men and women of the Commonwealth forces (consisting of the UK together with countries that were previously part of the British Empire) who died in the First and Second

World Wars, and ensures they will never be forgotten. This website provides a brief biography of each casualty together with details of where they are buried, with options to download "Commemorative Certificate" and "Cemetery Plan."

This website reveals that George Mitchell is buried in Amara War Cemetery in Iraq – which contains 4,621 burials of World War I – in Plot 21, Row K, Grave number 13. You can then view on this website a cemetery plan of Amara War Cemetery to identify exactly where George is buried.

The National Archives of Ireland holds a collection of 9,000 wills of Irish soldiers who died while serving in the British Army. Most of these date from World War I but there is a small number from the late 19th century and from the period of the South African War, 1899-1902. The documents have been digitized and can be examined online at the National Archives Genealogy Website at **www.genealogy.nationalarchives.ie** by selecting "Soldiers' Wills, 1914-1918."

WORKHOUSE RECORDS

During the Famine (1845-1852) over one million people died of starvation, fever and dysentery (including 20% of those who emigrated) and at least 1.25 million fled the country, the great majority to North America, some to Australia and a significant minority (over 300,000) to British cities. About 200,000 of the ill, hungry and destitute were accepted into the workhouses.

A report in the *Londonderry Sentinel* of 15 July 1848 confirms that during the Famine years children were sent from the workhouse in Derry to Australia:

"EMIGRANTS FROM THE LONDONDERRY WORKHOUSE TO AUSTRALIA –
On Tuesday, 27 young girls, accompanied by an elderly female, from the Londonderry Workhouse, embarked in the steamer *John Munn*, via Liverpool, to Dublin, from whence they will proceed to Plymouth, and sail for Australia, under the government grant of emigration. Their appearance does much credit to Miss McCandless, the matron, under whose superintendence their outfit was prepared, and has won for herself 'golden opinions' by her kindness and affability."

Records relating to workhouses in Ireland are part of Poor Law Records and the archives of the Board of Guardians. Poor Law Unions were the divisions or districts created by the Irish Poor Law Act of 1838. The country was divided into 130 unions, with a further 33 added after the Famine. Each Poor Law Union, consisting of a group of townlands, was named after a chief town in the district, and usually serviced the area in a ten-mile radius, often extending across county boundaries. Each Poor Law Union constructed a workhouse. As well as workhouses, the Board of Guardians maintained infirmaries and fever hospitals. The system was financed by a rate set by the Poor Law Valuation (i.e. Griffith's Valuation).

If people could not support themselves, they could come into the workhouse where they would do some work in return for food. People had to stay and live in the workhouse, and so the system was known as indoor relief. Life in the workhouse was meant to be harsh so as not to encourage people to stay; family members were split up into separate quarters.

The Boards of Guardians, created by the Irish Poor Law Act of 1838, were elected by rate-payers to oversee the administration of the Poor Law Union. Generally, they were local magistrates (landlords and their agents), wealthier tenant farmers and merchants. Following the partition of the island in 1922 the Guardians were abolished in Ireland in 1925, being replaced by County Boards of Health. Some workhouses were turned into district hospitals while others fell derelict. In Northern Ireland, the workhouse system lasted until the introduction of the Welfare State in 1948.

There is a comprehensive set of records covering Poor Law Unions. Classes of records include:

- Minute books
- Admission and Discharge Books
- Birth and Death Registers
- Outdoor Relief Registers

Survival of such records, however, for each of the unions varies from place to place.

One form of outdoor relief was the practice of putting out to nurse or boarding out orphan and deserted children. Under Acts of 1898 and 1900 a record of children and nurses had to be kept. You may find details either in the outdoor relief registers or in separate boarding-out registers.

As a result of the introduction of outdoor relief, the workhouses in Ireland had by 1900 become a refuge for the old, the sick and destitute children.

Public Record Office of Northern Ireland holds extensive records for the 28 Poor Law Unions that originally operated in the area now covered by Northern Ireland. Owing to the sensitive nature of some of the material contained within them, some records will be closed for 100 years from the latest date in each volume. Registers over 100 years old (where available) are open to the public.

In the Republic of Ireland the records associated with each Poor Law Union appear to be held at the appropriate County Council Library or Archive service. Again many of these offices may impose a closure period of up to 100 years for records identifying individuals.

By selecting "Workhouse Locations" on "The Workhouse: The story of an institution" website at **www.workhouses.org.uk**, you will find lists every Irish Poor Law Union, by county, and a brief history, accompanied by a map and photographs, of each workhouse together with summary details of surviving records and where they are held.

Findmypast, **www.findmypast.com**, is currently working in partnership with Irish archives and record offices to create a resource of all surviving Irish workhouse and Poor Law Union records. For example, they have digitized and indexed the Admission and Discharge Registers of Dublin workhouses for the time period 1840-1919, which contains over 1.5 million records. In these registers you can find out names, ages and religion as well as finding out previous address, occupations and the names of other family members.

THE REGISTRY OF DEEDS

The Registry of Deeds, located in Henrietta Street, Dublin, is undoubtedly a very useful source, as it holds a variety of records relating to property transactions, such as leases, wills, marriage settlements and other deeds, dating back to 1708.

A sworn copy, or "memorial," of the deed was presented at the Registry of Deeds in Dublin, not the original deed, which after registration was returned to the relevant solicitor or agent. On registration, the memorial was retained, given a reference number and indexed in a Name Index and, prior to 1947, in a Land Index. The memorial provides the fullest statement of the contents of a deed that the Registry holds.

While the original purpose of the Registry of Deeds was to enforce rules limiting the land transactions of Catholics, even before the removal of these rules in 1782 many Catholics and representatives of Catholic families appear in the memorials. Many memorials were registered by merchants and traders, as well as landed gentry, to provide some form of security of tenure.

Although the most common transaction registered was the lease, and most farms in Ireland were held by lease, there is no guarantee that an ancestor's lease or property transaction was registered. As deeds were only registered when the interested parties elected to do so, there is no means of predicting the existence of a deed. As a general rule small farmers and cottiers rarely figure in registered deeds, whereas merchants, traders and substantial farmers were more likely to figure in deeds.

Furthermore, the original indexes to the deeds, by name of grantor (i.e. name of landlord) and by place, were complicated to use. It is now, however, feasible to search this complex source, owing to the transcription work of the Registry of Deeds Index Project Ireland at **http://irishdeedsindex.net/search/index.php**.

For example, an examination of this index returns nine search results for the surname Hillhouse. These included:

Memorial Number 82070: Deed of Assignment of 'Estate of Freehall, and the Maine in co Londonderry' from Abraham Hillhouse senior, Gentleman to his son Abraham James Hillhouse junior, dated 16 September 1745.

Memorial Number 119,409: Abraham James Hillhouse, merchant of London, on 16 December 1758, leased and released 'Freehall & the Main, co Londonderry' to David Latouche of city of Dublin.

Memorial Number 123,629: Marriage settlement, dated 17 February 1757 of Abraham Hillhouse, Gentleman of Freehall, co Londonderry to Ann Ferguson, daughter of Rev Andrew Ferguson, of Burt, co Donegal of 'dowery out of Moneyvennon commonly known by Freehall and Upper & Lower Main, & live in the mansion house of Freehall in her widowhood.'

Hence, an examination of this source confirms that the Hillhouse estate at Freehall in Aghanloo Parish, near Limavady, County Derry passed, in 1745, from Abraham Hillhouse to his son Abraham James Hillhouse, who was a merchant in London, and that in 1757 Abraham Hillhouse of Freehall married Ann Ferguson, daughter of Reverend Andrew Ferguson of Burt, County Donegal.

ESTATE RECORDS

The pattern of great family estates established with the confiscations, plantations and settlements in the period to 1703 remained largely unchanged until they were finally broken up in the latter years of the 19th century under the Land Acts. Most of the acreage of Ireland was held in large estates. In 1871, 19 estates varied in size from 50,000 to 160,000 acres, 254 were in the range of 10,000 to 50,000 acres, while 418 were of 5,000 to 10,000 acres. These estates, because of their size, were run on a business basis in which records had to be kept of tenants' leases, rent payments and other such matters. Three records in particular are of great genealogical value, namely leases, rent receipt books and surveys. I will deal with each in turn.

Leases

Most Irish land was held by lease and, until the end of the 18th century, the most common form of lease seems to have been that for three lives. A lease for lives meant that the tenant qualified as a freeholder and was thus entitled to vote, which tended to strengthen the political "interest" of the landlord. The lives mentioned in the lease, of course, provide a great deal of useful genealogy. On the death of the longest living of the three stipulated lives, the lease would expire. The lease below, commencing on 1st November 1779, for William Patton's farm in Carrickananny, County Armagh, didn't expire until the death of John Patton on 3rd May 1857.

"This indenture made 28 September 1781 between the Right Honourable Lord Gosford and William Patton of the townland of Carrickanany in the County of Armagh.

"In consideration of the yearly rent, duties, covenants and agreements herein Lord Gosford doth demise, grant, set and to farm let unto the said William Patton and his heirs all the farm of land in the townland of Carrickanany now in the actual possession of William Patton containing by estimate 43 acres 3 roods 10 perches English statute measure together with 1 acre 20 perches of turf bog only granted for firing for the uses of the permises. All which concern are situate in the parish of Loughgilly, barony of Fews and County of Armagh. Lord Gosford reserves a full liberty of opening a road through said farm should he think it necessary.

"To hold for and during the life of Robert Patton now about 16 years old, also for and during the life of John Patton now about 14 years old, also for and during the life of George Patton now about 11 years old (3 sons of the lessee William Patton) or for and during the life of the longest lives of them commencing from 1 November 1779.

"The said William Patton paying every year the rent of £8 11s 1d, together with 12 pence per pound receivers fee, together with the carriage of 4 barrels of coal to be brought in good sound sacks either from Newry or Tyrone Coal pits as Lord Gosford shall please to appoint. And in case of refusal to go when called upon or not delivering the full measure at the mansion house at Gosford Castle to forfeit 4s 4d in lieu of each barrel of coals not delivered.

"And the said William Patton covenants for himself and his heirs that within 3 years from the date hereof he will enclose at least 1 acre of said premises for an orchard … and there plant apple trees in lines 31 feet by 21 feet asunder (The apple tree to be furnished by Lord Gosford with William Patton to pay Lord Gosford's gardener one halfpenny for each apple tree)….

"William Patton, his heirs and their under tenants shall grind all their corn, malt, grain at one of the manor mills belonging to Lord Gosford and shall pay the toll thereof.

"Obliged to ditch said farm as far as his Mearings Run with a sufficient ditch 6 feet wide and 5 feet deep and also to divide his farm into convenient fields with ditches 4 feet by 5 feet and to set in the face of all the ditches so made one row of white thorn or Crab tree quicks at the distance of 4 inches one quick from the other. And also to plant the face of such ditches so made with Oak, Ash or Elm at the distance of 21 feet asunder.

Signed and sealed by Lord Gosford and William Patton."

The following family tree can be deduced from the above lease:

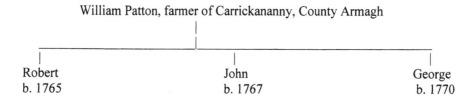

William Patton, farmer of Carrickananny, County Armagh

| Robert b. 1765 | John b. 1767 | George b. 1770 |

In addition to this genealogical information, a lease provides interesting information on the conditions attached to the granting of it. For example, Lord Gosford expected William Patton to enclose his farm, bound fields with neat hedgerows, plant an orchard, use the manor mill to grind grain, and carry coal to Gosford Castle.

Records of leaseholders also exist for towns as well as for large rural estates. For example, the Charter of 1613, which renamed Derry as Londonderry, obliged the landlord, the Irish Society of the city of London, to build a walled town. By 1619 the city was completely enclosed within a stone wall, 24 feet high and 18 feet thick.

The Irish Society laid out a town with about 300 house "lots" or "burgage plots." The plan of the new town, within the walls, was of a functional grid pattern. From the four central gates, the four principal streets met in an open area or diamond. All other streets then met the main streets at right angles. Housing extended along both sides of the main streets, with long narrow gardens behind. Outside the walls, gardens were also laid out from the walls to the river Foyle. By May 1628, 265 houses had been built inside the walls and leased to 155 families. These details are all recorded in a Rent Roll dated 15 May 1628.

Archives relating to the Irish Society are held in London Metropolitan Archives (**www.cityoflondon.gov.uk/things-to-do/london-metropolitan-archives/Pages/default.aspx**).

This archive contains surveys that name all leaseholders against their house lots within the walled city of Derry from the early years of the 17th century. These surveys include the rent roll of 1628, John Lane's Survey of 1695, Archibald Stewart's Survey of 1738 and J. C. Beresford's survey of 1826. This means that all leaseholders within the walled city are named and that changes in ownership of property over time can be identified.

In the original laying out of house "lots," leaseholders were also allocated a garden of 34 perches (i.e. about one quarter of an acre) outside the walled city but still located on the island of Derry (i.e. that area bounded by the River Foyle and the Bogside), and a farm of 4 or 6 acres in size in the Liberties of Londonderry. Thus, the occupiers of houses within the walls had a garden just outside the walls and a farm in the liberties surrounding the city. In its early years the city of Derry was a farming enterprise as well as a center of commerce and business.

Rent Receipt Books

When rent receipt books, kept by the landlord or his agent, extend over a lengthy period of time, it is often possible to follow changes in farm occupation. For example, the rent receipt book for Lord Gosford's Armagh estate shows that sometime between November 1822 and May 1823, Robert Patton died as his wife began to pay the rent:

Rent Receiving Book – Armagh Estate

Name	Robert Patton	Widow Patton
Townland	Carrickanany	Carrickanany
Account No.	416	416
Rent	£9 14s 9½d	£9 14s 9½d
For half year to	November 1822	May 1823

Surveys

Landlords quite frequently commissioned surveys of their estates, which were often accompanied by maps identifying tenants' holdings.

In 1821 William Greig submitted a report to Lord Gosford on the state of his 8,000-acre estate in County Armagh. Greig collected information on every holding on the estate and mapped them. The value of such a survey can be gauged by the fact that 3,000 people lived within the area so surveyed.

Greig's map of William Patton's lease, described previously, is produced below and shows that William Patton's original lease of 43 acres in 1779 was, by 1820, subdivided into seven farms. The map, furthermore, names the farmers.

The survey provides the following description against the above lease:

Farm No. 10 William Patton senior – now held by his sons Robert, George, and John and their sub tenants. Scarce any improvement seems to have been made on this farm.
> John Patton resides in Carrowmannon.
> George is only resident sometimes.
> Robert occupies the corn mill and has lately built a good flax mill but he and his family seem most slovenly.

This farm at the expiration of the lease might be let in 3 divisions. Only 2 divisions would be profitable. George doesn't deserve any part the buildings on his part are in the most ruinous condition and he seldom occupies much of the land himself.

William Patton's lease in farm no. 10:

Arable	42a 1r 10p
Chapel yard & mill dam	1a 2r 20p
Total	43a 3r 30p

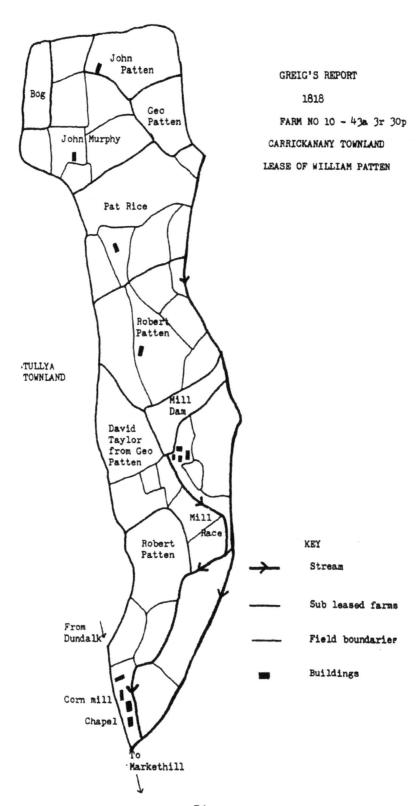

GREIG'S REPORT

1818

FARM NO 10 - 43a 3r 30p

CARRICKANANY TOWNLAND

LEASE OF WILLIAM PATTEN

John Patten

Bog

Geo Patten

John Murphy

Pat Rice

TULLYA TOWNLAND

Robert Patten

Mill Dam

David Taylor from Geo Patten

Mill Race

Robert Patten

From Dundalk

Corn mill

Chapel

To Markethill

KEY

Stream

Sub leased farms

Field boundaries

Buildings

74

In addition to this background material about each leased farm (i.e. farm size measured in acres, roods and perches), the survey provides quite detailed genealogical information on each family on the estate:

CARROWMANNON

Family	John Patton age 45
	Wife age 40
	4 children – 3 boys age 10 to 17 and 1 girl age 5
Servants	1 man
	1 maid
	1 cottier
Religion	Protestant
Character	Rather slovenly but opulent

It is clear that the amount of information, both genealogical and historical, that can be gleaned from surveys such as Greig's are immense. Greig highlighted two problems on the Gosford estate that give some idea of conditions existing in 19th-century Ireland. One was the high level of rents, based on a prosperous linen industry rather than on the productive capacity of the land, and the other was the substantial subdivision of holdings. John Patton's lease of 25 acres in Carrowmannon, for example, was sublet to five farmers who were also linen weavers with nine looms among them. The report states that these sub-tenants were "very industrious but excessive rents made them very poor and in great arrears to Patton."

If you know the townland your ancestor lived in or farmed, and the name of their landlord, then you should consider an examination of any relevant estate records. The Public Record Office of Northern Ireland (PRONI) holds the largest collection of estate records in Northern Ireland which are detailed, by county, in their *Guide to Landed Estate Records*. You can also search their eCatalogue online for relevant estate papers by accessing their website at **www.nidirect.gov.uk/services/search-pronis-ecatalogue**.

Landownership evolved over time as freeholds were granted and as landlords sub-let or sold their estates to middlemen. The "Immediate Lessors" column in Griffith's Valuation, at **www.askaboutireland.ie/griffith-valuation**, provides insight into landownership in Ireland in the middle years of the 19th century.

William Roulston's *Researching Scots-Irish Ancestors: The essential genealogical guide to early modern Ulster, 1600-1800* also provides detailed descriptions of 250 estate collections, in alphabetical order by estate (usually surname of the landlord), for each of the nine counties of Ulster.

In Republic of Ireland, collections of estate records are held in Dublin in both the National Library of Ireland and National Archives. Useful starting points to explore these collections are:

- Irish Landed Estates, Rentals and Maps in the National Library of Ireland at **www.nli.ie/en/irish-landed-estates-rentals-and-maps.aspx**.

- Guide to family and landed estate collections in the National Archives of Ireland at **www.nationalarchives.ie/article/guide-landed-estate-records**.

National University of Ireland, Galway has created the Landed Estates Database, at **www.landedestates.ie**, which provides a guide to landed estates and historic houses in the provinces of Connacht and Munster in the time period 1700 to 1914.

ORDNANCE SURVEY MEMOIRS

As a prelude to a nationwide valuation of land and buildings in Ireland, the so-called Griffith's Valuation, in 1824 the Ordnance Survey was directed to map the whole country. The resultant maps, at a scale of six inches to one mile, appeared between 1835 and 1846. In Griffith's Valuation, every townland in Ireland was identified against an Ordnance Survey sheet number.

The original intent was to accompany each map with written topographical descriptions for every civil parish. The compilation of these "Memoirs" commenced in 1830. By the time the idea was abandoned in 1840, only one, the parish of Templemore, County Derry, was published. Each parish was meant to take up no more than six pages of commentary; Templemore, which includes the city of Derry, needed 350 pages and the £1,700 cost was three times the original budget for the whole county! Furthermore, the publication of Samuel Lewis' two-volume *A Topographical Dictionary of Ireland* in 1837 (which can be examined at **www.libraryireland.com/topog**) weakened the case for the Memoirs. This publication provided "historical and statistical descriptions" of the "counties, cities, boroughs, corporate, market, and post towns" and "parishes, and villages" of Ireland.

The field officers of the Ordnance Survey, however, did gather a wealth of historical, geographical, economic and social information for many parishes in their notebooks. All the original manuscripts are deposited in fifty-two boxes in the Royal Irish Academy in Dublin (**www.ria.ie**). They cover twenty of Ireland's counties: Counties Antrim and Derry contain by far the most detailed information with seventeen and twenty boxes, respectively. Counties Donegal, Down, Fermanagh and Tyrone each account for two or three boxes, whereas the remainder, Counties Armagh, Cavan, Cork, Galway, Leitrim, Leix (formerly Queen's County), Longford, Louth, Mayo, Meath, Monaghan, Roscommon, Sligo and Tipperary have only one or part of one box each.

The Memoirs have been described as "a veritable doomsday book of the years 1830-40," offering a unique insight into life in Ireland immediately before the Great Famine (1845-1849). They can also provide useful genealogical information, as in many instances, emigrants, farmers, school teachers and mill owners are named.

The Memoirs for Counties Antrim and Derry are unique in that for many of their parishes lists of emigrants were compiled for a brief period in the 1830s. As emigration records these lists are unparalleled, identifying both the destination of the emigrant and their place of origin (townland address). In addition, the age, year of emigration and religious denomination are given for each emigrant. These lists record 1,922 emigrants from County Derry in the years 1833-1835 and 849 from County Antrim for the years 1833-1839. These emigrant details were published in *Irish Emigration Lists, 1833 – 1839: Lists of Emigrants Extracted from the Ordnance Survey Memoirs for Counties Londonderry and Antrim* (Genealogical Publishing Company, Baltimore, 1989)

The Memoir for the parish of Tamlaght Finlagan, County Derry records that a Presbyterian family from the townland of Ballymore, consisting of John Stewart, age 40, his wife Jane, age

40 and seven children, William 16, John 14, Robert 12, Jane 10, Elizabeth 8, Maryann 6 and Hugh 1, immigrated to Philadelphia in 1834.

The Memoir for the parish of Loughgilly, County Armagh, compiled in 1838, records that Sarah Patten was the occupier of a flax mill and a corn mill in the townland of Carrickananny, both powered by water wheels.

The Memoir for the parish of Seagoe, County Armagh records that the field officer visited Carrick female school on 28th November 1837. It was described as a mud cottage in the townland of Lemaghery, attended by 59 pupils of which 41 were under 10 years of age and 18 from 10 to 15; 52 pupils were Protestant [Church of Ireland], 1 Presbyterian and 6 Roman Catholic, and the school mistress was Anne Burrel.

The first systematic transcription, editing and publication of the parish Memoirs for Northern Ireland and the Border Counties of Ireland (Cavan, Donegal, Leitrim, Louth, Monaghan and Sligo) was undertaken between 1990 and 1998, in 40 volumes, by the Institute of Irish Studies at The Queen's University of Belfast (**www.qub.ac.uk/schools/IrishStudiesGateway**).

In 2002 the Institute published a 770-page index, covering all place and personal names in the 40-volume series; *Ordnance Survey Memoirs of Ireland: Index of People and Places* provides over 100,000 entries for people and places, indicating the parish, county, volume and page number of each reference.

Insights
and
Strategies

IRISH ADMINISTRATIVE DIVISIONS AND PLACENAMES

The key to unlocking Irish family history lies in knowing your ancestors' place of origin.

From a family historian's perspective, the most effective way to view Ireland is as a country that is subdivided into counties, which in turn are subdivided into parishes, and which in turn are subdivided into townlands. There are 32 counties, 2,508 civil parishes, and 60,642 townlands in Ireland.

Realistic genealogical research, in the absence of indexes and databases, generally requires knowledge of the parish in which your ancestor lived. Church of Ireland parishes normally conform to the civil parish, though Roman Catholic parishes do not, as they are generally larger. The Roman Catholic Church, owing to the Reformation of the 16th century, had to adapt itself to a new structure centered on towns and villages. The Presbyterian Church doesn't have a parish structure, with the congregations generally forming where there was sufficient demand from local Presbyterian families.

Researchers can identify Ireland's network of civil parishes by accessing the website **www.johngrenham.com/places/civil_index.php** and identify Roman Catholic parishes at **www.johngrenham.com/places/rcmap_index.php** by selecting county of interest on the displayed map of Ireland.

By using *A New Genealogical Atlas of Ireland* (2nd edition, Brian Mitchell, Genealogical Publishing Company, Baltimore, 2002) civil parish locations can be translated into Church of Ireland parishes, Roman Catholic parishes and Presbyterian Congregations (in province of Ulster). Presbyterian congregations in Ireland are very much associated with the nine counties of the northern province of Ulster.

A driving force among most people tracing their family history is to identify an ancestral home; to stand on land where the family house would have stood centuries ago. In Ireland this, in effect, means identifying the townland your ancestor lived in.

The single most important tool in identifying Irish placenames is the *Townland Index*, full title *General Alphabetical Index to the Townlands and Towns, Parishes and Baronies of Ireland* (Alexander Thom, Dublin, 1861; reprinted by Genealogical Publishing Company, Baltimore, 1984). It is a record of townland names, their size and location – by county, barony, civil parish, Poor Law Union and 1st edition Ordnance Survey map number – as recorded in the 1851 census and as they have been officially spelled and designated ever since.

You can also search the *Townland Index* online, together with street listings from Dublin, Cork and Belfast cities, to pinpoint county, civil parish and Poor Law Union locations for more than 65,000 placenames in Ireland, by visiting **www.johngrenham.com/places** and choosing the "placename" search option.

Between 1829 and 1842 Ordnance Survey Ireland completed the first ever large-scale survey of an entire country. These maps were surveyed on a county basis. Hence, a record of townland names, shapes and sizes for all Ireland exist in these maps at a scale of six inches to one mile.

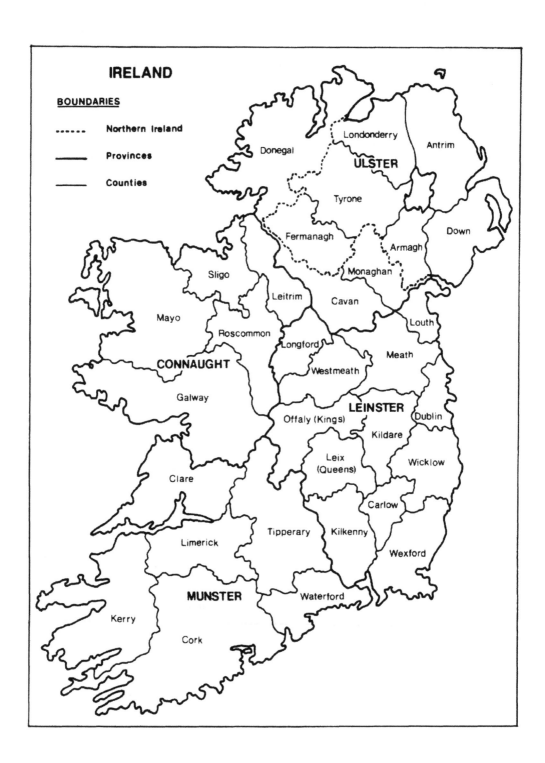

IRELAND

BOUNDARIES

..... Northern Ireland

——— Provinces

——— Counties

CIVIL PARISHES

Ballywillin

Bally-aghran

Dunboe

Tamlaghtard

Kill-owen

Coleraine

Ballyra-shane

Kildoll-agh

Ballymoney

Formoyle

Aghanloo

Macosquin

Agivey

Drumachose

Aghadowey

Tamlaght Finlagan

Balteagh

Errigal

Faughanvale

Carrick

Desertoghill

Kilrea

Templemore

Bovevagh

Bovevagh

Tamlaght O'Crilly

Clondermot

Cumber Lower

Dungiven

Killelagh

Maghera

Cumber Upper

Banagher

Bally-scullion

Learmount

Termoneeny

Maghera

Ballynascreen

Kilcronaghan

Desertmartin

Magherafelt

Artrea

Lissan

Desertlyn

Derryloran

Tamlaght

Ballinderry

81

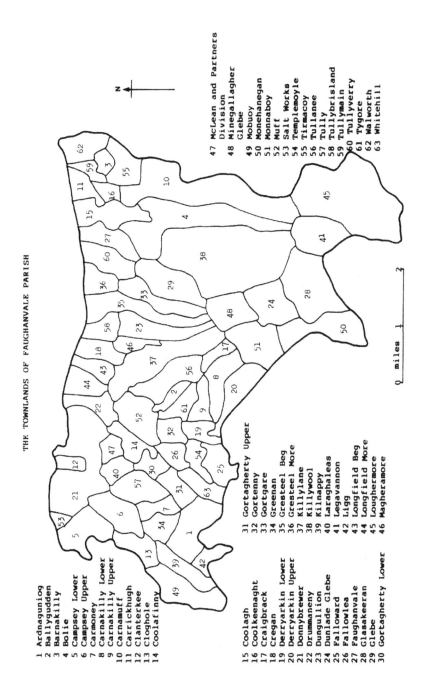

THE TOWNLANDS OF FAUGHANVALE PARISH

1 Ardnaguniog
2 Ballygudden
3 Barnakilly
4 Bolie
5 Campsey Lower
6 Campsey Upper
7 Carmoney
8 Carnakilly Lower
9 Carnakilly Upper
10 Carnamuff
11 Carrickhugh
12 Clanterkee
13 Cloghole
14 Coolafinny

15 Coolagh
16 Coolkeenaght
17 Craigbrack
18 Cregan
19 Derryarkin Lower
20 Derryarkin Upper
21 Donnybrewer
22 Drumananeny
23 Dungullion
24 Dunlade Glebe
25 Falloward
26 Fallowlea
27 Faughanvale
28 Glasakeeran
29 Glebe
30 Gortagherty Lower

31 Gortagherty Upper
32 Gortenny
33 Gortgare
34 Greenan
35 Gresteel Beg
36 Gresteel More
37 Killylane
38 Killywool
39 Kilnappy
40 Laraghaleas
41 Legavannon
42 Ligg
43 Longfield Beg
44 Longfield More
45 Loughermore
46 Magheramore

47 McLean and Partners Division
48 Minegallagher Glebe
49 Mobuoy
50 Monehanegan
51 Monnaboy
52 Muff
53 Salt Works
54 Templemoyle
55 Tirmacoy
56 Tullanee
57 Tully
58 Tullybrisland
59 Tullymain
60 Tullyverry
61 Tygore
62 Walworth
63 Whitehill

0 miles 1 2

Townlands vary greatly in area as their size was generally based on the fertility of the land. In Faughanvale parish, which contains 66 townlands, the fertile lowland townland of Muff is some 318 acres in size, while Killywood, which extends into the Loughermore Hills, contains 1,471 acres. The townland was loosely based on the ancient Irish land measure called the ballyboe, which means cow townland. As a ballyboe was based on the area that could support a fixed number of cattle, it is not surprising that its size varied depending on land quality.

82

Table of Irish Administrative Divisions

The following administrative divisions form the geographical basis for genealogical research. Records of value to the family historian were gathered by one or more of these divisions.

Administrative Division	Description
PROVINCE	The largest geographical division. Ireland is divided into 4 provinces: Connacht, Leinster, Munster and Ulster.
COUNTY	Ireland is divided into 32 counties. This division, begun in the 12th century, reflected the imposition of the English system of local government in Ireland. Their boundaries reflected the lordships of the major Gaelic families.
BARONY	This subdivision of a county is now an obsolete division, but in the 19th century it was widely used. Ireland was divided into 327 baronies which tended to reflect the holdings of Irish clans. Baronies and counties became established in the government land surveys of the 17th century.
PARISH	From the 17th century the so-called civil parish, based on the early Christian and medieval monastic and church settlements, was used extensively in various surveys. There are 2,508 civil parishes in Ireland. Most record sources of value, both civil and church, to family historians were compiled and recorded by parish. Ecclesiastical parishes were grouped into **dioceses**.
TOWNLAND	The smallest and most ancient land division in Ireland. Parishes were, in effect, subdivided into townlands, a few hundred acres in extent. There are 60,462 townlands in Ireland. In identifying a townland address you have effectively identified the ancestral home.
POOR LAW UNION	Districts, centered on a large market town, created in 1838 for the financial support of the poor. Ireland was originally divided into 130 Poor Law Unions. In 1898 the Poor Law Union replaced the civil parish and barony as the basic unit of local government. Poor Law Unions were subdivided into 829 **Registration Districts** (to gather civil birth, marriage and death details) and 3,751 **District Electoral Divisions** (to gather census returns).
ESTATE OR MANOR	In 17th, 18th and 19th centuries, until they were finally broken up in the latter years of the 19th century under the Land Acts, the majority of the population of Ireland lived on large estates. The administration of these estates by landlords and their agents produced a large quantity of records, including maps, rentals, account books, leases, title deeds and surveys.
PROBATE DISTRICT	Created in 1858 for the purpose of proving wills. There were 12 probate districts in Ireland.

You can view modern, satellite and historic maps – including 6-inch maps (1837–1842) and 25-inch maps (1888–1913) – of townlands of Ireland with the Ordnance Survey of Ireland Map Viewer at **http://map.geohive.ie/mapviewer.html**.

For the townlands of Northern Ireland, you can view historic maps – including first edition (1832–1846), second edition (1846–1862), third edition (1900–1907), and fourth edition (1905–1957) Ordnance Survey maps – together with modern maps and aerial photographs by accessing the Public Record Office of Northern Ireland's Historical Maps viewer at **www.nidirect.gov.uk/services/search-proni-historical-maps-viewer**.

Irish Placenames

A database of administrative placenames (townlands, parishes, names of urban centers, etc.) for Ireland, in both Gaelic and English, can be searched in "The Placenames Database of Ireland" at **www.logainm.ie**.

At **www.placenamesni.org** you can identify the location, origin and meaning of over 30,000 placenames from all over Northern Ireland.

Inconsistency in spelling of placenames is well known to those who have conducted research into their Irish family history. An "official" and standardized recording of townland names for all Ireland was established, by 1842, by the Ordnance Survey and published in the *Townland Index* and the maps of the Ordnance Survey.

Placenames, originally in Gaelic, were anglicised from the 17th century, by settlers with little knowledge of the Irish language. This resulted in a number of different spellings of the same place name. For example, in Clondermot parish, County Derry, the townland which was standardized as Coolkeeagh in the *Townland Index* and the maps of the Ordnance Survey was recorded as Killkeeraugh in the 1831 census and as Culkeeragh in the Tithe Book of 1834.

On the east bank of the River Faughan in Faughanvale parish, County Derry, there is an area that prior to the 17th-century Plantation of Ulster, was called by Irish speaking inhabitants as *Camsan*, meaning "the winding of a river." It was anglicized as Campson Lower and Campson Upper by 17th-century surveyors; and, in the 1830s, it was described as Campsie Lower and Campsie Upper (arising from a popular myth of a connection to 1689 Siege of Derry hero, Lieutenant Henry Campsie) and then mapped "officially" as Campsey Lower and Campsey Upper by Ordnance Survey engineers!

It must also be pointed out that there are many placenames in Ireland (some of which appear on maps and others that don't) that are even more localized than a townland name. In 1991 the Federation for Ulster Local Studies published *Every Stoney Acre has a name: a celebration of the Townland in Ulster*.

Seoirse Ó Dochartaigh, a Gaelic-speaking musician, artist and genealogist, has spent many years talking to local people (and listening to how they pronounce placenames) and viewing old maps to compile a comprehensive list of placenames and their derivation, by townland, in Inishowen, County Donegal. The results of this research were published, in 2011, in *Inis Eoghain: The Island of Eoghan: The Place-Names of Inishowen*.

Seoirse, for example, identifies 452 placenames within the 30 "official" townlands and one island (Glashedy) that make up the civil parish of Clonmany! Gaelic society was highly complex and organized. English administrators from early 1600s divided Inishowen into a collection of quarterlands (which became the new townlands) and grouped them into parishes, ignoring larger Gaelic land units such as ballybetaghs or tuatha and smaller ones such as ballyboes and sessiaghs.

An examination of Valuation maps and 1st edition Ordnance Survey maps confirms that, in the mid-19th century, in many rural areas, and in particular in marginal areas less suited to profitable farming, the population was still living in small village clusters that had not yet been broken up into the dispersed farm dwellings that dominate the Irish landscape today. Such clusters of farmhouses in "farm towns" without church, shop or public house were called clachans. Historically, clachans were the nuclei of Ireland's network of townlands.

Seoirse records that older people in Clonmany still call a townland a quarterland and refer to the smaller clusters within it as the townlands. Bally (Baile), found in placenames all over Ireland, derives from a cluster of houses; it doesn't refer to a town in the modern sense. Baile means a homestead or gathering of people. Clusters of houses, i.e. clachans, were part of ancient communal farming systems involving three or four generations of one family, and the land around the clusters was further subdivided into three or four ballyboes or grazing shares, sometimes called townlands. Ballyboes were sometimes further subdivided into six sessiaghs or plough shares.

It is clear from an examination of 19th-century maps that the townland of Tullagh (711 acres in size) in Clonmany parish at one time consisted of seven townlands, with village settlements named as Ballynagolman, Drumshee, Fallbane, Hilltown, Kindrohid, Norway and Tullagh. Prior to the breakup of these clachans into dispersed farms, residents of Norway, for example, would have considered Norway, not Tullagh, as their townland.

Seoirse records that Norway is derived from Gaelic *An Fharaire*, meaning the stony shore. The fact that Norway is named in 1st edition Ordnance Survey map (completed by 1842) dispels a lovely story I was once told about the origin of this placename; in the 1850s a Norwegian ship was wrecked off Tullagh Point and some of the crew settled here, hence that part of townland of Tullagh became known as Norway!

If you can't find an Irish placename you are looking for, there are two major reasons for this:

1.
The placename you seek is spelled differently than the "official" spelling. It is only in comparatively recent times, i.e. from the mid-19th century, that attempts have been made to standardize the spelling of Irish placenames.

2.
Although the townland is the smallest and most ancient of Irish land divisions – there are 60,462 townlands in Ireland – and is effectively equated with identification of the ancestral home, it is quite possible that the placename you seek is even more localized than a townland name.

SURNAMES AND IRISH IDENTITY

An exploration of the history of an ancestor's surname is a useful first step on a journey to tracing roots in Ireland. Although only detailed family history research will confirm the actual origins of an ancestor, surname histories can provide clues and insight into family history.

Surnames, as they are very much connected to place in Ireland, are an integral part of Irish identity and family history. Pride in Irish roots is often reflected, and indeed reinforced, in pride in surname, or an ancestor's surname, which confirms a connection with Ireland.

For example, McLaughlin is the second most common surname (after Doherty) in Derry city today. Tracing their lineage to Eoghan, son of the 5th century High King of Ireland, Niall of the Nine Hostages, the McLaughlins, from their homeland in Inishowen, County Donegal, became High Kings of Ireland in the 12th century and patrons of the monastic settlement in Derry. From the mid-13th century the O'Neills of Tyrone ousted the McLaughlins as the leading power in Ulster.

Many families in Derry, Donegal and Tyrone trace their lineage to Eoghan and Conall *Gulban*, sons of Niall of the Nine Hostages. Eoghan and his brother Conall *Gulban* conquered northwest Ireland, c. 425 AD, capturing the great hill-fort of Grianan of Ailech, which commanded the entrance to the Inishowen peninsula, County Donegal.

Doherty, a variant of O'Doherty, is by far the most popular name in Derry city today. This County Donegal sept, which originated in Raphoe, but settled in Inishowen from the 14th century, can trace their lineage to Conall Gulban, son of Niall of the Nine Hostages. They ruled Inishowen until the arrival of an English army at Derry in 1600. An O'Doherty-led rebellion, which included the ransacking of Derry in 1608, helped pave the way for the Plantation of Ulster.

Sources

An excellent starting point for surname research is the Irish Ancestors website at **www.johngrenham.com/surnames**, as its "Surname search" option enables you to examine the location, frequency and history of Irish surnames.

I also refer to the following surname reference books to build up a picture of the location and history of Irish surnames:

- *The Surnames of Ireland* by Edward MacLysaght (Irish Academic Press, Dublin)
- *All Ireland Surnames* by Sean de Bhulbh (Comhar-Chumann Ide Naofa Teo, Limerick)
- *The Book of Ulster Surnames* by Robert Bell (Blackstaff Press, Belfast)
- *A Dictionary of Surnames* by Patrick Hanks and Flavia Hodges (Oxford University Press)
- *The Surnames of Scotland: Their Origin, Meaning, and History* by George F. Black (The New York Public Library)

Surname Variants

Inconsistency in spelling of surnames is well known to those who have conducted research into their Irish family history. You will find that in the context of Irish historical records there are many spelling variations of the same name. Anglicization of Gaelic names, together with illiteracy, resulted in numerous spelling variations of the same name and, in some cases, the adoption of inappropriate surnames. Many surnames in historic documents will be based on a phonetic spelling of what the record compiler heard. And on top of this, many records were made by officials with no knowledge of Gaelic speech.

There is no doubt that the process of anglicization has obscured the origins of many Irish surnames. From the 17th century Gaelic surnames of Irish and Scottish origin were translated, and in many cases mistranslated, into English; others were changed to similar-sounding English names. Family names of Gaelic origin were further disguised in the 18th century by discarding the prefix Mac, Mc and O.

For example, Smith may be a surname of English or Scottish origin or the anglicization of Gaelic McGowan (meaning son of Smith). Many surnames in the Derry area, such as Clarke, Green, Mitchell and Rodgers, could have originated independently in England, Scotland or Ireland; only detailed family history will confirm the actual origin.

Thus, in conducting family history research you should be aware of the possibility of different spellings of the same surname. For example, variant spellings of Doherty, derived from Gaelic *O Dochartaigh*, to name but a few, include Daugherty, Docherty, Dogherty, Dougherty, O'Doagharty, O'Dogherty and O'Doherty; and of Rosborough, with origins in Scotland, include Rosborrow, Rossboro, Rossborough, Roxberry, Roxborough, Roxbrough and Roxburgh.

Studies of Surname Distribution

In the 17th century substantial numbers of English and Scottish families settled in the northern part of Ireland during the so-called Plantation of Ulster. These settlers came to Ulster, by and large, in three waves: with the granting of the initial leases in the period 1605 to 1625; after 1652 and Cromwell's crushing of the Irish rebellion; and, finally in the 15 years after 1690 and the Glorious Revolution.

Studies of surname distribution – based on an examination of 17th- and 18th-century census substitutes such as the Muster Rolls of 1630, Hearth Money Rolls of 1663 and Protestant Householders Lists of 1740 – can shed useful light on the nature of English and Scottish settlement in 17th-century Ulster.

Such studies tend to support the view that the evolution of predominantly English or Scottish settlement areas in Ulster was established from the earliest days of the 17th-century Plantation of Ulster.

These studies also show, as evidenced by marked changes in the actual individual surnames at any location between the 1630 Muster Rolls and Hearth Money Rolls of the 1660s, that from the earliest days of the Plantation there was a high level of internal mobility and population turnover.

An examination of 17th- and 18th-century census substitutes supports the claim that after 1700 Protestant settlement in Ulster was formed by internal movements of population rather than by further emigration from England or Scotland.

They also illustrate that farm occupancy, based on the townland, established in the 17th century when land was relatively plentiful, established areas of Planter/Irish settlement that generally survive to this day. As a generalization, if a townland didn't have a relatively large number of British settlers in occupation by 1740 it never became dominated by them, since the native Irish were then able to establish themselves.

It is clear that the analysis of surname distribution, in Irish census records and census substitutes of the 18th century and earlier, is an important tool in migration research.

For example, although the bulk of lands in Faughanvale parish, County Derry belonged to either the Grocers' or Fishmongers' Companies of the City of London, an examination of the Hearth Money Rolls of 1663 and of the Protestant Householders Lists of 1740 confirms the influx of predominantly Scottish settlers into the fertile lands of Faughanvale parish, centered on the village of Eglinton, in the middle and latter part of the 17th century. The results of this examination are summarized in the tables below.

Planters settled in Faughanvale Parish by 1663

Surname	Firstname	Townland
Ash	John	Killylane
Barrett	William	Fallalea
Bigger	James	Gresteel Beg
Clide	Robert	Greysteel
Corcherane	George	Monabuoy
De Lappe	James	Cloghole
Donnelsonn	John	Ligg
Gottra	Archibald	Faughanvale
Henry	Archibald	Campsey
Huestone	John	Tully
Kinkead	John	Magheramore
Kirkwood	Robert	Gresteel More
Mac Farlan	Donnell	Tullanee
Mccleland	Patrick	Managh
Moore	John	Carnamuff
Patterson	John	Coolkeeagh
Robb	James	Managh
Robinson	Robert	Kilnappy
Rosse	Anthony	Fallalea
Temple	James	Ballygudden
Thompson	Thomas	Ballygudden
Sterling	James	Gresteel Beg
Williams	John	Cregan
Wilson	Andrew	Ardinagonnage

Scottish Planters settling in Faughanvale Parish after 1690

Surname	1663	1740	Number of References in 1740
Archibald	No	Yes	1
Campbell	No	Yes	2
Cowan	No	Yes	4
Craig	No	Yes	3
Gillespie	No	Yes	3
Gilliland	No	Yes	4
Inch	No	Yes	2
Jameson	No	Yes	1
Kitchen	No	Yes	5
Mackey	No	Yes	2
Miller	No	Yes	3
Morrison	No	Yes	2
Murray	No	Yes	3
Parkhill	No	Yes	2
Scoby	No	Yes	1
Scott	No	Yes	1
Stewart	No	Yes	3

Although these sources name heads of household only, they are very useful in confirming the presence of a family name in a particular area, and in providing some insight into the frequency and distribution of surnames. As most surnames can tentatively be identified as being English, Scottish or Irish in origin, an examination of these census substitutes can prove very illuminating in highlighting the spread of English and Scottish settlers into Ulster.

In the case of Faughanvale parish it is clear that Scottish Planters dominated the settler population, and that the big influx of Scottish settlers to the area came after 1691 and the cessation of the Williamite Wars in Ireland.

IRISH PASSENGER LISTS

Official passenger lists from Ireland only exist from 1890, and they are held in the Board of Trade records (reference BT27) in the National Archives, Kew, London (**www.nationalarchives.gov.uk**). Now digitized and indexed (at **www.ancestry.com** and **www.findmypast.com**) these lists name 24 million long-haul passengers who left from 35 ports in the United Kingdom (which includes the Republic of Ireland until partition in 1921) between 1890 and 1960. On finding a passenger of interest, you can then download and print the passenger manifest.

These passenger departure lists, from 1922, record the address in Ireland of all embarking passengers; prior to this the only clue to family origin was either "Nationality" (e.g. Irish, Scottish, English) or "Country of Last Permanent Residence."

As a general rule, prior to 1890 you are more likely to identify passengers at the port of arrival as opposed to the port of departure. You should, therefore, check the website of the appropriate National Archives: National Archives and Records Administration in the United States at **www.archives.gov**; Library and Archives Canada at **www.collectionscanada.gc.ca**; National Archives of Australia at **www.naa.gov.au**; Archives New Zealand at **www.archives.govt.nz**; and National Archives and Records Service of South Africa at **www.national.archives.gov.za**.

In the U.S. official arrival records of immigrants were kept from 1820. Ancestry's "US Immigration Collection" (**www.ancestry.com**) contains indexes to passenger lists of ships arriving from foreign ports to Boston from 1820 to 1943 (3.8 million immigrants); Philadelphia, 1800 to 1945 (1.6 million); and New York, 1820 to 1957 (82 million). Information contained in the index includes: given name, surname, age, gender, ethnicity, nationality or last country of permanent residence, destination, arrival date, port of arrival, port of departure and ship name. Furthermore, the names found in the index are linked to actual images of the passenger lists.

The "US Immigration Collection" also names 16.3 million passengers arriving in the U.K. (from foreign ports outside of Europe) between 1878 and 1960; 8.4 million "unassisted" immigrants to New South Wales, Australia from 1826 to 1922 and 450,000 "assisted" immigrants to New South Wales from 1828-1896; and 7.3 million passengers arriving at Canadian ports between 1865 and 1935.

The Immigrant Ships Transcribers Guild has transcribed over 18,000 passenger manifests on their website **www.immigrantships.net**.

By the mid-19th century, 70% of Irish emigrants entered the U.S. through New York. The emigrant landing depot at Castle Garden, run by New York State's Board of Emigration Commissioners, received 8 million immigrants from 1855-1890. It was replaced by a new federal immigration station at Ellis Island in 1892, which between 1892 and 1924 received 12 million immigrants. "The Port of New York Passenger Records 1820 – 1957" database contains the passenger lists of almost 65 million immigrants, passengers, and crew members who came through Ellis Island and the Port of New York from 1820 to 1957, and these can be searched, free of charge, at **www.libertyellisfoundation.org/passenger**.

"The Londonderry to Philadelphia route" was the oldest Irish emigrant trade route to North America. By the 1820s Derry had become the leading city in Ireland in dealing with pre-paid passages. Irish immigrants in America found it easier to pay a ship's captain or an agent for passages for their friends and relatives in Ireland rather than sending money direct to them.

In 1802 DuPont's gunpowder works was established at Hagley along the banks of the Brandywine in Wilmington, Delaware, and almost from the start the Company helped its workforce to send for their families and friends in Ireland. Most of the ships that were used and the agents that handled the DuPont Company accounts were based in Philadelphia, thus the story of the DuPont immigrants is intertwined in the bigger story of Irish immigration and the port of Philadelphia.

The fantastic range of digital sources relating to the DuPont Company at the Hagley Museum and Library, at **www.hagley.org/research/digital-exhibits/sources**, sheds light on the Company's role in arranging passage for emigrants through Irish ports, and through the port of Derry in particular.

For example, in one letter, dated 24th February 1832, Robert Taylor, the agent for the Company in Philadelphia, writes to DuPont, "agreeably to your second letter of the 23rd instant, handed me by Patrick McIlhenny, I have given him an order for two passages from Londonderry to this Port, together with my Bill on James Corscaden & Co. of L.Derry in favour of Bernard McIlhenny for four pounds sterling."

The memo at the bottom of this letter states:

"From L.Derry to Philadelphia	Bernard McIlhenny	$28
	Biddy McIlhenny	$28
	Bill for £4.0.0. Sterling	$21
	Total	$77"

In other words, DuPont was being billed $77 to cover the passage cost, arranged by Robert Taylor, of Bernard and Biddy McIlhenny, at $28 each, and remittance of £4 to be sent to Bernard McIlhenny in Ireland. Such Bills of Exchange, in this case drawn on James Corscaden & Co, merchant and shipowner of 26 Shipquay Street, Derry, enabled friends and relatives in the United States to send money to relatives in Ireland.

This payment by DuPont was effectively a fringe benefit on offer to their employees. In this case, it enabled Patrick McIlhenny, who was working at DuPont's gunpowder works, to be reunited with his brother, Bernard, and sister, Biddy, long before it would have been possible otherwise. Patrick could not have raised $77 in one lump sum, but through the benevolence of DuPont he was able to pay back in monthly instalments to the Company the passage fare and money advance.

In terms of surviving passenger departure lists from Ireland, prior to 1890, the port of Derry is unique, in that four different sources, which include government papers, government surveys and business records of shipping firms, name immigrants to North America in the years 1803-1806, 1833-1839 and 1847-1871. They have been indexed and published in three books by the Genealogical Publishing Company, Baltimore: The details of these books are as follows:

- *Irish Passenger Lists, 1803 – 1806: Lists of Passengers Sailing from Ireland to America Extracted from the Hardwicke Papers.*
- *Irish Emigration Lists, 1833 – 1839: Lists of Emigrants Extracted from the Ordnance Survey Memoirs for Counties Londonderry and Antrim.*
- *Irish Passenger Lists, 1847 – 1871: Lists of Passengers Sailing from Londonderry to America on Ships of the J. & J. Cooke Line and the McCorkell Line.*

18th-Century Irish Passenger Lists

Between 1718 and the beginning of the War of American Independence in 1776, 250,000 emigrants left the province of Ulster, through the ports of Belfast, Londonderry, Newry, Larne and Portrush, for the British Colonies in North America. Researchers wishing to explore this story further should read R. J. Dickson's *Ulster Emigration to Colonial America 1718-1775* (published by the Ulster Historical Foundation, Belfast).

According to Sir Edward Newenham, prominent member of the Dublin Parliament, in the five-year period from July 1769 to July 1774, 152 ships sailed for the Colonies in North America, carrying an estimated 43,020 emigrants from Ulster. The breakdown being: 50 sailings from Derry; Belfast 43; Newry 38; Larne 16; and Portrush 5.

No official passenger departure lists from Ireland exist for this period. However, a database of published arrival records to North America in the 17th, 18th and 19th centuries has been compiled in the "Passenger and Immigration Lists Index, 1500s-1900s." This index to 5.4 million immigrants who arrived in United States and Canadian ports from the 1500s can be accessed in the "US Immigration Collection" at **www.ancestry.com**.

Immigrant arrival records can be reconstructed to some extent by an examination of records relating to land grants in 18th-century Colonial America. Many 18th-century emigrants from Ulster came to North America in search of land to farm.

For example, *History of Londonderry*, by George Franklin Willey (Londonderry, New Hampshire, 1975), includes "Map of a large portion of the original town of Nutfield settled in 1719 and chartered as Londonderry in 1722, prepared and drawn by Revd. J G McMurphy," which names and maps the earliest settlers of Londonderry, New Hampshire. Reverend James MacGregor, minister of Aghadowey Presbyterian Church, County Derry (near Coleraine), had accompanied some of his congregation to Boston and they established, in 1719, the settlement of Londonderry, New Hampshire.

Indeed, the names of 35 of the earliest settlers of Londonderry, New Hampshire are the names of those who signed a petition, dated 26 March 1718, in which 311 "inhabitants of the North of Ireland" (including 12 Presbyterian ministers) appointed Reverend William Boyd of Macosquin Presbyterian Church, County Derry (near Coleraine) to negotiate a grant of land from Samuel Shute, governor of New England. They were:

Surname	First Names
Alexander	James & Randall
Blair	John
Caldwell	William
Campbell	William
Clark	John
Cochran	Andrew & John
Craig	David, James & John
Gray	John
Gregg	James
McKeen	James, John & Robert
Miller	Robert
Mitchell	John
Moore	James & John
Morrison	James
Nesmith	James
Patterson	James
Rodgers	James
Smith	James
Thompson	James & John
Wallace	William
Wear	Robert
Wilson	James, John, Robert, Thomas & William
Woodburn	John

David Dobson's prolific collection of books, published by Clearfield Company, Baltimore, can be seen as an invaluable attempt to reconstruct lists of emigrants and of emigrant ships that crossed the Atlantic from Ireland to North America in the 18th century.

Based "mainly on contemporary newspapers and archival sources in Canada, the United States, UK and Ireland," David Dobson has compiled, in nine volumes, *Irish Emigrants in North America* that "documents the departure of thousands of individuals who left Ireland for the promise of the New World between roughly 1670 and 1830."

In his four-volume series of books, *Ships from Ireland to Early America 1623-1850*, by using contemporary newspapers on both sides of the Atlantic together with some government records and published books, David Dobson lists, in alphabetical order by name of ship, "vessels from Ireland known or likely to have been carrying passengers." For example, an examination of these books identifies 26 ships that sailed from Ireland to North America in 1719: 14 destined for Boston, Philadelphia 6; Charleston 4; New York 1; and Amboy, New Jersey 1.

An examination of newspapers on both sides of the Atlantic can shed much light on the emigration process as well as details about emigrant ships and individual emigrants.

In Northern Ireland there are two newspapers still in publication today that were established in the 18th century and were based in the two cities, Belfast and Londonderry, which were the major embarkation points for Irish emigrants to North America throughout the 18th century.

The *Belfast Newsletter* is the oldest English language general daily newspaper still in publication in the world, having first been printed in 1737. As details of ships sailing to America were advertised in local newspapers, an index to the *Belfast Newletter* from 1737 to 1800, compiled by John C. Greene, can be searched at **www.ucs.louisiana.edu/bnl**. The 18th-century index to this Northern Irish newspaper contains nearly 300,000 items of news and advertisements.

The *Londonderry Journal* (known today as the *Derry Journal*) has been in continuous publication since 1772. In *Irish Genealogical Abstracts from the Londonderry Journal, 1772-1784*, Donald M Schlegel (published by Clearfield Company, Baltimore) has abstracted all notices of marriages, births, deaths, and persons immigrating to North America that appeared in this newspaper between 1772 and 1784.

An examination of the *Londonderry Journal* can, for example, help piece together the last voyage of the ship *Faithful Steward*.

The *Faithful Steward* departed Derry for Philadelphia with 249 passengers (and 13 crew) and a cargo of linen and casks of copper coins (this was before the U.S. had a mint for small circulation coins) on 9 July 1785 and was shipwrecked on 1 September 1785 at the entrance to Delaware Bay within 100 yards of land (known as Coin Beach today from coins washed ashore from the shipwreck). There were 68 survivors, including all crew members.

Londonderry Journal of 20 April 1784 reported that Abraham McCausland, merchant of Culmore, Londonderry and Captain Conolly McCausland, mariner and merchant of Streeve Hill, Limavady had purchased two thirds of the ship *Stewart,* 300 tons, from Archibald Stewart of Providence, Rhode Island, and the ship was renamed *Faithful Steward.*

News reached Derry of the loss of this ship, tens weeks after the disaster, as *Londonderry Journal* of 15 November 1785 published "a brief account of the unfortunate disaster which befel the Ship Faithful Steward, Conolly McCausland, Master, from London-Derry, bound to this port [Philadelphia]; taken from a Gentleman who was passenger on board."

The survivors, 68 in total, consisting of 13 "Ship's Crew," 10 "Cabin Passengers," and 45 [steerage] "Passengers," were named in *Londonderry Journal* of 21 February 1786.

Today, the historic content of a wide range of Irish provincial newspapers can be searched at the British Newspaper Archive at **www.britishnewspaperarchive.co.uk** and Irish Newspaper Archives at **www.irishnewsarchive.com**. For example, Irish Newspaper Archives has indexed and digitized the *Belfast Newsletter* from 1738, while the British Newspaper Archive has indexed and digitized the content of the three newspapers that served 19th-century Derry city: *Derry Journal* 1825-1955, *Londonderry Sentinel* 1829-1959 and *Londonderry Standard* 1836-1872.

"The Irish Emigration Database" – compiled by the Mellon Centre for Migration Studies at the Ulster American Folk Park, Omagh, County Tyrone – is a virtual library of emigration-related primary sources, principally letters to and from emigrants dating from c. 1780 to c. 1920; it can be searched at **www.dippam.ac.uk**. This extensive collection of more than 33,000 records is drawn from a number of collections, including the Public Record Office of Northern Ireland and many private donors.

DNA AND GENETIC GENEALOGY

It is very difficult to trace ancestors in Ireland through the 18th century owing to patchy survival of record sources for this time period. The majority of Irish church registers, which are essentially the building blocks of Irish family history, don't survive for the 18th century. Hence the birth, marriage and death details of many of our 18th-century ancestors are not recorded in a written record source. It is quite possible, for example, even in the first half of the 19th century, that the baptism you seek occurred before its written confirmation in a surviving church register. This means that unless your family history has been documented and passed down through the generations you have limited means to confirm family connections.

Once you have exhausted traditional genealogical sources, if you can find no potential "matches" in the "big" Irish family history websites and you hold no clues as to county/parish of origins of your ancestors within Ireland, I believe you then have to take a step backwards and attempt to reach out to a wider family history community in the hope that you can make contact with someone with knowledge/oral traditions that may not be found in any historical documents and/or captured in any database but may shed new light on the origins of your ancestors.

A growing number of people are purchasing DNA tests in the hope that they can make contact with "genetic cousins" whose DNA test results "match" and who may hold more information about the family tree than they currently hold, either in the form of historical documentation or oral tradition as to the origins of a family.

I do believe there is a role for DNA in genealogy but it requires much work (i.e. contacting potential matches) and luck (that one of the matches holds "new" information about family origins, either in the form of historical documentation or oral tradition).

In Ireland Dr Maurice Gleeson has a growing reputation both for his knowledge about DNA testing and genetic genealogy and as an advocate "for using DNA as a genealogical tool to help you break through those frustrating family-tree brick walls." Further information, including contact details, will be found at **https://dnaandfamilytreeresearch.blogspot.com/p/courses-consultations.html**.

In Northern Ireland Martin McDowell, Education and Development Officer with the North of Ireland Family History Society (NIFHS), is an enthusiast about the benefits of DNA testing. Martin is one of the administrators of the North of Ireland DNA Project with FamilyTreeDNA (FTDNA), and he is keen to promote DNA testing across Ireland (contact and further details at **www.nifhs.org/dna**).

DNA is the genetic code that resides in every cell in the body. Your ancestry is written in your DNA as you get half your DNA from your mother and half from your father; a quarter from each of your four grandparents; one eighth from each of your great-grandparents; and so on.

There are three main types of DNA Tests for Family Historians:

- mtDNA is passed down from mothers to their children. It is therefore a useful marker in tracking back along the mother's maternal line. mtDNA test provides a list of matches who share common direct ancestry within 52 or more generations. It is widely used in Migration Studies to track movements of modern humans out of Africa (50,000 years ago) and in studies of "Ancient DNA." It is the least useful of the three main DNA tests for genealogists.

- Y-DNA is only passed from father to son and is very useful for tracing back along the direct male line. Y-DNA test provides a list of matches who share common direct paternal ancestry within 25 generations. It is very useful for surname studies because Y-DNA, like surnames in Ireland, is inherited along the male line.

- Autosomal DNA test (atDNA) is the most popular of the three main types of DNA tests and is the most useful genealogically. This test can connect you with genetic cousins on all of your ancestral lines (male and female). atDNA test provides a list of matches who share common ancestors from any of your ancestral lines within the past five generations. It also gives you information about your ethnic makeup, i.e. what percentage of your DNA came from different places. The test has become more refined and can now predict down to country level in some places and soon will be able to predict down to a regional level in some countries such as U.K. and Ireland. You will also learn of your connection with ancient migration groups. Seemingly, three major groups of people have had a lasting effect on present-day peoples of European descent: Hunter-Gatherers, who migrated into Europe during an inter-glacial period, 45,000 years ago; Stone Age farmers who migrated here after the last Ice Age, 8,000 years ago; and Bronze Age invaders who introduced copper tools from 3,000-1,000 BC.

DNA Testing Companies:

- AncestryDNA, **www.ancestry.com/dna**
- FamilyTreeDNA, **www.familytreedna.com**
- MyHeritage DNA, **www.myheritage.com/dna**
- 23andMe DNA, **www.23andme.com**
- Living DNA, **www.livingdna.com**

AncestryDNA claims that it brings together "DNA technology" with "millions of family trees" and "billions of historical records." For example, AncestryDNA matches are cross-checked against Ancestry's unrivalled database of family trees.

Which DNA test?

- If you are particularly interested in researching your surname, you should consider getting a Y-DNA test and join the relevant surname project.

Dr Tyrone Bowes argues that you can use Y-DNA to pinpoint your Irish "Genetic Homeland" on the Irish Origenes Surnames of Ireland map at **www.irishorigenes.com** and identify those surnames that occur as a genetic match to you.

The "Genetic Homeland" is the location where one's ancestors lived for hundreds of years; it is the area where they first took their surname, where they left their mark in placenames and in the DNA of its current inhabitants. Over 1,000 years ago, when surnames were adopted, groups of related individuals gave rise to a small number of surnames that arose in a specific location within Ireland. Hence people with different surnames today can share common ancestry.

Thus, surname matches from Y-DNA testing can be a snapshot of your ancestor's neighbours from 1,000 years ago. Since Irish surnames can still be found concentrated in the areas where they first arose, one can examine surname distribution maps and see where in Ireland those surnames originate and reveal a "Genetic Homeland."

- If you want a more general test that will help you explore all of your ancestral lines, then do the Autosomal DNA test.

Points to consider when analysing atDNA test results:

- Always remember that atDNA results are a statistical estimate of percentage of DNA you share with a "genetic cousin," with specific ethnic groups and with the ancient peoples of Europe.

- One scientist has claimed that DNA ancestry tests are no more than "genetic astrology." Ethnicity testing is the least reliable aspect of DNA testing, as the estimate of your genetic ethnicity is based on comparing your DNA to the DNA of other people who are native to a region. Owing to wars, famines, migrations and invasions, the population of continents and countries have changed over time, so there is no such thing as a representative sample of the indigenous population as "we are one big mixing bowl"!

- The list of matches you get are of genetic cousins with whom you share a common ancestor at some stage within the last 200 years or so. Through your own family history research and by contacting your matches, you can then begin to figure out where the connection is in your respective family trees. For example, if the test says that you are likely to be 3rd cousins, that means you probably share a set of great-great-grandparents in common with each other, and you will then need to compare your trees and see if the same set of great-great-grandparents appear in both trees.

- The reach of the atDNA test is limited to about the level of your great-great-great-great-grandparents. The amount of DNA you inherit from any single 4xgreat-grandparent is very small, only about 1.5%. This is because the amount of DNA is halved with each subsequent generation. (Each parent passes on 50% of their DNA to a child; hence you share 25% of your DNA with a grandparent, 12.5% with a great-grandparent, 6.25% with 2xgreat-grandparent and 3.125% with 3xgreat-grandparent).

DNA testing is only a tool to aid genealogical research; its value depends on a significant pool of people, with knowledge of their family tree, sharing this information with genetic matches. DNA tests are very dependent on who else has signed up. If a cousin is not on the DNA database of the company that you tested with, then you won't be linked up. You could potentially search for near relations and come up with nothing. From a genealogical point of view the bigger the pool of people you can match with, the better the chance of making a connection with someone who is connected to you.

Testing with one company only allows you to compare results with that particular company's database; so, it does make sense to test with one company, say AncestryDNA, and then transfer your data results to another testing company, such as FamilyTreeDNA. That way you can compare results with the data pools of the big two DNA testing companies.

You may also wish to consider registering, by providing a valid email address, with GEDmatch, at **www.gedmatch.com**, as this website provides applications for comparing your DNA test results with other people. GEDmatch users can upload their autosomal DNA test data from commercial DNA companies to identify potential relatives who have also uploaded their profiles.

THE MAJOR RECORD OFFICES OF IRELAND

General Register Office
Government Offices, Convent Road, Roscommon, F42 VX53, Ireland
Telephone: +353 (0)90 663 2900
Website - **www.groireland.ie**
Email - **gro@groireland.ie**

The General Register Office is the central civil repository for records relating to births, marriages and deaths in Ireland.

Irish Civil Records of births, marriages, and deaths can now be searched and viewed at **www.irishgenealogy.ie**. Records are searchable by name, event type, year and name of Superintendent Registrar's District; a pdf of the full register page in which that birth, marriage or death certificate appears can then be downloaded by selecting "image." At present, images are available for Births 1864-1919, Marriages 1845-1944, and Deaths 1878-1969. Further register images of Deaths 1864-1877 will follow later. The website's civil records cover the entire island up to and including 1921. From 1922 on, it does not hold records registered in the six counties of Northern Ireland.

General Register Office for Northern Ireland
Colby House, Stranmillis Court, Belfast, BT9 5RR, Northern Ireland
Telephone: +44 (0)300 200 7890
Website: **www.nidirect.gov.uk/gro**
Email: **gro_nisra@finance-ni.gov.uk**

The General Register Office for Northern Ireland is the central civil repository for records relating to births, marriages and deaths in Northern Ireland.

You can search and view "historic" civil records of births (over 100 years old), marriages (over 75 years old) and deaths (over 50 years old) for Northern Ireland at GRONI Online, **www.nidirect.gov.uk/services/go-groni-online**.

National Archives of Ireland
Bishop Street, Dublin 8, D08 DF85, Ireland
Telephone: +353 (0)1 407 2300
Website: **www.nationalarchives.ie**
Email: **query@nationalarchives.ie**

The National Archives of Ireland is the official repository for the state records of Ireland.

A varied selection of databases for Ireland – such as 1901 and 1911 Census Returns, surviving Census Returns (1821-1851), Census Search Forms (1841/1851) of Old Age Pension applicants, Tithe Applotment Books (1823-1837), Will copies and indexes (1596-1920), Marriage License Bonds Indexes (1623-1866), Catholic Qualification and Convert Rolls (1700-1845), Valuation Office Books (1824-1856), Shipping Agreements and Crew Lists (1860-1921), and Soldiers' Wills (1914-1918) – can be searched at the National Archives Genealogy website at **www.genealogy.nationalarchives.ie**.

The National Archives also offers a free Genealogy Advisory Service. Further details at **www.nationalarchives.ie/genealogy/free-genealogy-advisory-service**.

National Library of Ireland
7-8 Kildare Street, Dublin 2, D02 P638, Ireland
Telephone: +353 (0)1 603 0200
Website: **www.nli.ie**
Email: **info@nli.ie**

The National Library's holdings constitute the most comprehensive collection of Irish documentary material in the world. *Sources: A National Library of Ireland Database for Irish Research*, at **http://sources.nli.ie**, contains over 180,000 catalogue records for Irish manuscripts, and for articles in Irish periodicals.

The Genealogical Office manuscript collections in the Office of the Chief Herald at National Library of Ireland are the most important source for the genealogies of Gaelic families and of those families entitled to bear arms either by hereditary right or by grant. The Chief Herald is responsible for the granting and confirming of coats of arms to individuals and corporate bodies. All arms granted are recorded in the Register of Arms, maintained since the foundation of the Office in 1552. The Register of Arms and other Genealogical Office collections, such as indexes to registered and unregistered pedigrees, can be accessed in the Manuscripts Reading Room in the National Library of Ireland. Further details about this office and its manuscript collections are available at **www.nli.ie/en/intro/heraldry-introduction.aspx**.

The National Library of Ireland also offers a free Genealogy Advisory Service. Further details at **www.nli.ie/en/genealogy-advisory-service.aspx**.

Public Record Office of Northern Ireland
2 Titanic Boulevard, Titanic Quarter, Belfast, BT3 9HQ, Northern Ireland
Telephone: +44 (0)28 9053 4800
Website: **www.nidirect.gov.uk/proni**
Email: **proni@communities-ni.gov.uk**

The Public Record Office of Northern Ireland (PRONI) is the official repository of public and private archives for Northern Ireland.

A varied selection of databases for Northern Ireland – such as Londonderry Corporation Records (1673-1901), 17th- and 18th-century Census Substitutes, pre-1840 Freeholders' Registers and Poll Books, Street Directories (1819-1900), Will indexes (1858-1965), copies of Wills (1858-1909), Valuation Revision Books (1864-1933), and Signatories to 1912 Ulster Covenant – can be searched at PRONI's online archive at **www.nidirect.gov.uk/information-and-services/public-record-office-northern-ireland-proni/search-archives-online**.

TRACING YOUR IRISH ANCESTORS: A THREE-STEP GUIDE

Background

There are 2,508 parishes in Ireland. You can identify the civil parishes of Ireland, and their associated townlands, at **www.johngrenham.com/places/civil_index.php** by selecting county of interest on the map. To gain insight into the economic and social landscape of 19th-century Ireland you can consult *A Topographical Dictionary of Ireland,* published in 1837, by Samuel Lewis. Arranged in alphabetical order by parishes, towns and villages, this book can be viewed online at **www.libraryireland.com/topog/placeindex.php**. An excellent starting point for surname research is the "Surname Search" option at **www.johngrenham.com/surnames** where you can explore the location, frequency and history of Irish surnames.

Research Steps

Step 1 - Search 1901 and 1911 Census Returns

Although census enumerations were carried out every decade from 1821, the earliest surviving complete return for Ireland is that of 1901. The census enumerations of 1901 and 1911, arranged by townland in rural areas and by street in urban areas, can be searched, free of charge, at **www.census.nationalarchives.ie**. These returns will list the names, ages and place of birth of all members in a household.

Step 2 – Search for births, marriages and deaths

Civil registration of births, deaths and Roman Catholic marriages in Ireland began on 1st January 1864 while non-Catholic marriages were subject to registration from 1st April 1845. Prior to the commencement of civil registration of births, marriages and deaths in Ireland, family history researchers usually rely on baptismal, marriage and burial registers kept by churches. With civil registration of births and deaths commencing in 1864, and with the patchy survival of church records prior to 1820, gravestone inscriptions can be a vital source for family historians.

Irish Civil Records of births, marriages and deaths can now be searched and viewed at **www.irishgenealogy.ie**. On searching the index, which returns name, event type, year and name of Superintendent Registrar's District, a pdf of the full register page in which that birth, marriage or death certificate appears can be downloaded by selecting "image." At present, images are available for Births 1864-1919, Marriages 1845-1944 and Deaths 1878-1969. Further images of Deaths dating back to 1864 will follow later.

RootsIreland, at **www.rootsireland.ie**, is a good starting point for searching church registers of baptisms, marriages and burials as this website is the largest online source of Irish church register transcripts. You can either search across all counties or search a particular county. For example, Derry Genealogy, at **www.derry.rootsireland.ie**, has transcribed and computerized the early baptismal and marriage registers of 97 churches (38 Roman Catholic, 24 Church of Ireland and 35 Presbyterian; the earliest being the registers of St. Columb's Cathedral in Derry city, which date from 1642) and gravestone inscriptions from 117 graveyards.

As the search facility on this website is very flexible, it means that you should be able to determine if any entries of interest to your family history are held on this database. For example, if you are searching for the baptism/birth of a child you can narrow the search down by year, range of years, names of parents and by parish of baptism/district of birth. Marriage searches can be filtered by year, range of years, name of spouse, names of parents and parish/district of marriage.

It must be stated, however, that a failure to find relevant birth/marriage entries in this database doesn't mean that the events you are looking for didn't happen in Ireland. It simply means that they are not recorded in the database; for example, they may be recorded in a record source that doesn't survive for the time period of interest or in a source that has not been computerized or, perhaps, in the database of another county.

For example, you can search, free of charge, at **www.irishgenealogy.ie**, Church of Ireland parish registers for Counties Carlow and Kerry and Dublin city; and Roman Catholic parish registers of County Kerry, Dublin city and west and south Cork (i.e. parishes in Dioceses of Kerry and Cork and Ross except most of Cork city).

Step 3 – Search Census Substitutes

Quite often the only realistic strategy in tracing ancestors beyond church registers (which are the building blocks of family history) is to examine surviving land records and census substitutes, often compiled by civil parish, for any references to a surname or given name of interest. The problem with these sources is that they name heads of household only; hence they provide insufficient information to confirm the nature of linkages between named people in these sources. Census substitutes, however, are very useful in confirming the presence of a family name in a particular townland and/or parish, and in providing some insight into the frequency and distribution of surnames.

You can examine the mid-19th-century Griffith's Valuation by visiting the website **www.askaboutireland.ie/griffith-valuation**; the early-19th-century Tithe Books at the website **www.titheapplotmentbooks.nationalarchives.ie**; and the 1796 Flax Growers' Lists at the website **www.failteromhat.com/flax1796.php**. It must be emphasized that such sources will confirm the presence of a name and/or surname of interest but they will not confirm if there is a connection between people with the same surname!

CASE STUDY: TRACING THE IRISH ANCESTRY OF ALDERMAN JAMES MCCARRON

In this case study, six steps are followed in researching the 19th-century family history of a former prominent citizen of the city of Derry, Alderman James McCarron.

1. Starting Point

Every family history quest begins with a story. In this case the starting point is of a now long-forgotten incident during the final month of the First World War.

James McCarron, Labour Leader and Alderman of Londonderry Corporation, was one of over 500 people drowned when RMS *Leinster* was torpedoed and sunk by German submarine UB-123 on 10 October 1918 while bound for Holyhead from Kingstown (known, from 1921, as Dun Laoghaire or Dunleary). The *Leinster* had on board 687 passengers and a crew of 70.

Official news had reached Derry on Friday 11 October 1918 that the Royal Mail Steamer *Leinster*, bound from Dublin to Holyhead, had been sunk.

An examination of the local newspaper, *Derry Journal*, quickly identified the death notice of James McCarron in the *Journal* of Monday 14 October 1918:

McCARRON – October 10, 1918, drowned in the s.s. Leinster, off Kingstown, James McCarron, alderman of this city. His remains will be removed from his late residence, 48, Stanley's Walk, Derry at 9.45 am today (Monday) for Requiem Mass in Long Tower Church. Funeral to the City Cemetery immediately afterwards.

On page 3 of the *Derry Journal* of 14 October 1918 fuller details were provided under the headline: "Death of Alderman J McCarron – Universal Feeling of Grief." It states that James McCarron was "one of the ablest and most respected Labour leaders in Ireland, and one of the best and most highly esteemed citizens of Derry." It also reported that "his remains were conveyed to Derry by the Great Northern train," which reached the city at 9.20 pm on Saturday (12th October) to be met by an "enormous gathering of citizens."

2. Search 1901 and 1911 Census Returns

At **www.census.nationalarchives.ie** you can now search, free of charge, the 1901 and 1911 census returns, which include images of original documents for all counties in Ireland. These returns, arranged by townland and parish in rural areas and street and town in urban areas, detail, for every person, their name, age, religion, education, occupation, marital status, and county or city of birth, or country (if born outside Ireland). The 1901 and 1911 census returns for the family of James McCarron were quickly identified on this website.

The 1901 census (enumerated "on the night of SUNDAY, the 31st of MARCH 1901") identified, in form B.4, the Roman Catholic household of James McCarron, a tailor, age 45 and his wife Margaret, age 43 and children Annie (18), M. Josephine (16), James (15), Elizabeth (13), Richard A. (10), Joseph (6) and Veronica (4) residing at "Lone Moor Road – Part of –

right hand side from Blees Lane" [spelled today as Bligh's Lane]. This return noted that James McCarron had been born in "County Derry" and that his wife and children in "Derry city."

The 1911 Census (enumerated "on the night of SUNDAY, the 2nd of APRIL 1911") recorded, in form B.47, the household of James McCarron, a tailor, age 59 and his wife Margaret, age 53 and children Annie (28), Elizabeth (23), Joseph (16) and Veronica (14) living at Stanley's Walk. Two grandsons of James McCarron were also listed; William Patrick McCarron, age 5, who was born in "Glasgow" and David McCarron, age 3, who was born in "Philadelphia USA."

Additional information provided in the 1911 census (which was not asked for in 1901) noted that Margaret had been married to James McCarron for 35 years and that she had given birth to fourteen children, ten of whom were still living.

It should be pointed out that any ages recorded in census returns should be used as a guide to deducing dates of birth. In the 1901 census James McCarron's age is recorded as 45, yet ten years later, in 1911, it is recorded as 59!

3. Search Civil Birth and Marriage Registers

Based on our examination of census returns we can now construct the following family tree:

- James McCarron was born c. 1852-1856, in County Derry.
- James' wife, Margaret (maiden name not known at this stage), was born c. 1858 in Derry City, and they married c. 1876.
- James and Margaret McCarron had 14 children; the names of 7 of whom are known (at this stage): Annie born c. 1883; M. Josephine born c. 1885; James born c. 1886; Elizabeth born c. 1888; Richard A. born c. 1891; Joseph born c. 1895; and Veronica born c. 1897.

It is now time to examine civil registers of births and marriages.

Civil registration of births, deaths and Roman Catholic marriages in Ireland began on 1 January 1864, while non-Catholic marriages were subject to registration from 1 April 1845. Derry Genealogy has computerized all pre-1922 civil birth and marriage registers for Derry city and surrounding districts and made them accessible online at **www.derry.rootsireland.ie**.

An examination of Derry Genealogy's database of civil birth registers confirmed that the maiden name of James McCarron's wife was Casey, as the civil birth details of the following children were recorded in Derry city (in Londonderry Urban Number 2 district) to parents James McCarron, tailor and Margaret Casey:

Child's Name	Birth Date	Birth Place
John	20 July 1876	Creggan Street
Mary	5 March 1878	4 Creggan Street
David	27 December 1880	6 Creggan Street
Annie	1 October 1882	12 Ann Street
Mary Josephine	25 May 1884	Elmwood Terrace
Sarah	28 February 1892	7 Stanleys Terrace
Sarah Kathleen	16 May 1893	4 Stanleys Terrace

You can also search, free of charge, civil registers of births 1864-1919, marriages 1845-1921 and deaths 1878-1921 for Northern Ireland at **www.irishgenealogy.ie**, which means that you can view, download and/or print scanned images of any or all of the above birth certificates for your family history folder.

According to the 1911 census James and Margaret McCarron had 14 children. Hence it would appear that the births of 7 of James McCarron's children were not recorded in civil birth registers!

However, as Derry Genealogy has also computerized all pre-1900 Roman Catholic baptismal registers for Derry city and surrounding parishes the "missing" children in civil birth registers were soon identified in church baptismal registers. Baptismal entries (but no civil birth entries) were found for the following additional children born to parents James McCarron and Margaret Casey:

Child's Name	Baptismal Date	Church
William	15 March 1879	St. Eugene's Cathedral
James	20 August 1885	St. Eugene's Cathedral
Elizabeth	19 May 1887	St. Eugene's Cathedral
Michael Joseph	15 July 1888	St. Eugene's Cathedral
Richard Alphonsus	20 April 1890	St. Eugene's Cathedral
Joseph	12 January 1895	Long Tower Chapel
Veronica	10 February 1897	Long Tower Chapel

Roman Catholic baptismal registers sometimes record marriage details against a child's baptismal entry. In this case, marriage details are recorded against one of James McCarron's sons: James McCarron (baptized 20 August 1885) was noted as having married Magdelina Burns in Chester, Pennsylvania, USA on 6 June 1910.

A search of civil marriage registers, which are available at either **www.irishgenealogy.ie** or **www.derry.rootsireland.ie**, identified James McCarron's marriage:

Church:	St. Columba's, Long Tower Roman Catholic Chapel, Derry city
Date:	16 May 1875
Groom:	James McCarron, tailor of Joseph Street
Bride:	Margaret Casey, factory girl of Creggan Street
Father of Groom:	John McCarron, labourer
Father of Bride:	Michael Casey, labourer
Witnesses:	James Doherty and Annie Ferguson

4. Search Church Baptismal and Marriage Registers

Based on our examination of census returns and of civil birth and marriage registers we can now speculate that:

- James McCarron was born c. 1852-1856 in County Derry to a father John McCarron
- Margaret Casey was born c. 1858 in Derry City to a father Michael Casey.

As births in Ireland were not subject to civil registration until 1864, further research will have to rely on church baptismal registers to confirm birth details of James McCarron and Margaret Casey. Dates of commencement and quality of information in church registers vary from parish to parish and from denomination to denomination. Access to church registers, in the absence of indexes and databases, is generally gained through knowledge of an ancestor's parish address and religious denomination.

Derry Genealogy has computerized all pre-1901 Roman Catholic church registers in Counties Derry and Donegal that are located within the Diocese of Derry. This database (at **www.derry.rootsireland.ie**) was examined and the baptismal details for James McCarron and Margaret Casey were found:

Church:	Coleraine Roman Catholic Parish (Diocese of Derry)
Baptismal Date:	28 March 1852
Child's Name:	James
Father:	John McCarron
Mother:	Easther McMullan
Sponsors:	Daniel McMullan and Anne Cunning

By visiting the website of the National Library of Ireland at **https://registers.nli.ie** you can also examine pre-1880 Roman Catholic registers for most parishes of Ireland. On selecting a parish you can then browse through a scanned copy of the original register, which formerly was only accessible on microfilm in the National Library of Ireland.

The Roman Catholic population of the civil parishes of Aghadowey, Agivey, Dunboe, Killowen and Macosquin in County Derry, to the west of Coleraine town, are served by the parish of Coleraine in the Diocese of Derry (the Roman Catholic parish for Coleraine town itself is located within the Diocese of Connor).

The registers of Coleraine Roman Catholic parish (Diocese of Derry) also detail the baptisms of two siblings of James McCarron; Catherine baptized 6 September 1857 and Thomas 4 July 1864.

It would appear that around 1850 the McCarrons moved to Coleraine parish from Magilligan parish as the following baptism was also identified:

Church:	Magilligan Roman Catholic Parish (Diocese of Derry)
Baptismal Date:	25 December 1849
Birth Place:	Carnowry
Child's Name:	Daniel
Father:	John McCarron
Mother:	Ester McMullan
Sponsors:	Charles McCarron and Mary Jane Quinn

It will be noted that the registers of Magilligan parish record townland addresses. The townland of Carnowry, 7 miles west of Coleraine town, sits right on the boundary of Magilligan Roman Catholic parish and is bounded to the east by Coleraine Roman Catholic parish and, in particular, by the chapel of St Mary's, Dunboe.

Margaret Casey's baptism, as expected, was identified in Derry city:

Church:	Long Tower Roman Catholic Chapel
Baptismal Date:	1 August 1855
Child's Name:	Margaret
Father:	Michael Casey
Mother:	Mary McGinley
Sponsor:	Eliza Doherty

Prior to 1873 and the opening of St. Eugene's Cathedral, the entire Roman Catholic population of Derry city, on the west bank of the River Foyle in the civil parish of Templemore, was served by St. Columba's, Long Tower Chapel.

The registers of Long Tower also detail the baptisms of four siblings of Margaret Casey: Elizabeth baptized 31 January 1857, Catherine 22 August 1858, Michael 19 October 1860, and Ellen 1 January 1867.

It would, therefore, appear that:

- John McCarron married Easther McMullan around 1848 or earlier
- Michael Casey married Mary McGinley around 1854 or earlier

Unfortunately Derry Genealogy's database of Roman Catholic Church registers doesn't record these marriages. This, therefore, raises the possibility that these marriages occurred in a church whose registers don't extend back far enough.

5. Search Griffith's Valuation

With church registers exhausted we now turn our attention towards the mid-19th-century Griffith's Valuation. Owing to the destruction of most 19th-century census returns in Ireland (from 1821 through to 1891), Griffith's Valuation is a record of extreme importance to family researchers. It is, in effect, a census substitute for post-Famine Ireland. Griffith's Valuation was a survey carried out for every parish in Ireland between 1848 and 1864, detailing every rateable head of household and occupier of land in Ireland by townland or street address. The results of the survey were published in volumes by Poor Law Union.

You can now search, free of charge, Griffith's Valuation for all Irish counties (which includes images of original documents and maps) by Family Name and Place Name at the website **www.askaboutireland.ie/griffith-valuation**.

It would be reasonable to assume that John McCarron (i.e. father of James) and Michael Casey (i.e. father of Margaret) may have been recorded as heads of households in this source in the Coleraine and Derry areas, respectively. Griffith's Valuation returns for the Poor Law Union of Londonderry, published in 1858, names householders and landholders who resided in Derry city and suburbs, while the returns for the Poor Law Union of Coleraine, published in 1859, names householders and landholders who resided in Coleraine town and suburbs.

An initial examination of Griffith's Valuation (viewable at **www.askaboutireland.ie/griffith-valuation**) failed to identify any McCarron households in those townlands located within the Roman Catholic parishes of Coleraine and Magilligan.

However, you will always find that in the context of Irish historical records there are many spelling variations of the same name. Thus, in conducting family history research you should be aware of the possibility of different spellings of the same surname. A re-examination of Griffith's Valuation identified a household headed by John McKearn residing, in 1859, in a house valued at 5 shillings, in the townland of Bennarees in the civil parish of Dunboe.

The townland of Bennaress is bounded to the west by the townland of Carnowry (i.e. where John and Easther McCarron were living at the time of the birth of their son Daniel in 1849). Furthermore, John McKearn's neighbor in Griffith's Valuation was one Daniel McMullen (we know from our research that John McCarron's wife was called Easther McMullen!).

It is, therefore, reasonable to assume, but not proven, that this John McKearn of Bennarees is the father of James McCarron (born 1852) and that Daniel McMullen of Bennarees is the father of Easther McMullen. In this period Sir Henry R. Bruce of Downhill Castle was the landlord of Bennarees.

Based on an examination of Griffith's Valuation it is also reasonable to assume that Creggan Street in Derry city was the birthplace of James McCarron's wife, Margaret Casey. There was only one household headed by a Michael Casey (i.e. the father of Margaret Casey) in all of Derry city at time of Griffith's Valuation; a household headed by Michael Casey was residing, in 1858, in "house and yard" valued at £2 15 shillings, on Creggan Street.

6. McCarron Surname History

As our journey into James McCarron's family history began with a story, it is only right that it should end with another.

Surnames are very much connected to place in Ireland and therefore are an integral part of Irish identity and family history. Pride in Irish roots is often reflected, and indeed reinforced, in pride in surname, or an ancestor's surname, that confirms a connection with Ireland. Those bearing the surname McCarron are, in all probability, linked to Counties Derry and Donegal and to a history that stretches back over 1,500 years.

The McCarron sept of Inishowen, County Donegal, trace their lineage to Eogan, son of the 5th-century High King of Ireland, Niall of the Nine Hostages, who ruled from the Hill of Tara (County Meath). By tradition, Eogan and his brother Conall Gulban conquered northwest Ireland, c. 425 AD, capturing the great hill-fort of Grianan of Ailech, which commanded the entrance to the Inishowen peninsula, County Donegal.

Ireland was one of the first countries to adopt a system of hereditary surnames, which developed from a more ancient system of clan or sept names. From the 11th century each family began to adopt its own distinctive family name, in general derived from the first name of an ancestor who lived in or about the 10th century. The surname was formed by adding the prefix Mac (son of) or O (grandson, or descendant of) to the ancestor's name. In its homeland, in Inishowen, McCarron was derived from Gaelic *Mac Cearáin*. Irish surnames are still very dominant and numerous in the very localities where their names originated. Hence, in the mid-19th century, 80% of the descendants of the McCarron sept in County Donegal were still living in Inishowen.

McCarron, which is a common surname in Derry city today, illustrates the close links, both historic and economic, between the city of Derry and the Inishowen district of Donegal. As Derry developed an industrial base in the 19th century in shirt making, shipbuilding and distilling, it attracted much of its workforce from Donegal. In the 90-year period 1821 to 1911 the population of the city quadrupled to 40,780.

In this particular instance it would appear that James McCarron's ancestors migrated to Derry city from Inishowen (County Donegal), via Magilligan (County Derry). In the years before the 17th-century Plantation of Ulster, with English and Scottish settlers, some of the original Gaelic families of Inishowen had migrated eastwards and settled in the lands of Magilligan, across Lough Foyle, beneath Binevenagh Mountain in north Derry.

SOURCES FOR TRACING 17TH- AND 18TH-CENTURY SCOTS-IRISH ANCESTORS

Definition of Scots-Irish

The term Scots-Irish refers to people whose ancestors, often Presbyterian, originated in Scotland and settled, during the 17th century, in Ireland in the nine northern counties of the Province of Ulster: Antrim, Armagh, Down, Fermanagh, Londonderry and Tyrone in Northern Ireland and Cavan, Donegal and Monaghan in the Republic of Ireland. They are also called Scotch-Irish or Ulster-Scots. Today, it is a matter of personal preference to refer to these people as Scotch-Irish, Scots-Irish or Ulster-Scots; in Northern Ireland they are generally referred to as Ulster-Scots and in the United States as either Scotch-Irish or Scots-Irish.

The Plantation of Ulster

In the 17th century substantial numbers of English and Scottish families settled in the northern part of Ireland during the so-called Plantation of Ulster. Movement of Scottish settlers in a private enterprise colonization of Counties Antrim and Down began in earnest from 1605 when Sir Hugh Montgomery and Sir James Hamilton acquired title to large estates in north Down and Sir Randall MacDonnell, 1st Earl of Antrim, to large tracts of land in north Antrim. In 1609 the Earl of Salisbury suggested to James I a more formal, deliberate plantation of English and Scottish colonists in Counties Armagh, Cavan, Donegal, Fermanagh, Londonderry (then known as Coleraine) and Tyrone.

These settlers came to Ulster, by and large, in three waves: with the granting of the initial leases in the period 1605 to 1625; after 1652 and Cromwell's crushing of the Irish rebellion; and finally in the 15 years after 1690 and the Glorious Revolution, when it is estimated that 50,000 people came to Ulster from Scotland. It is estimated that by 1715, when Scottish migration to Ulster had virtually stopped, the Presbyterian population of Ulster, i.e. of essentially Scottish origin, stood at 200,000.

18th-Century Emigrants

Between 1717 and the beginning of the War of American Independence in 1776, 250,000 Scots-Irish left Ulster, through the ports of Belfast, Londonderry, Newry, Larne and Portrush, for the British Colonies in North America. The Scots-Irish tended to enter America through Philadelphia and they headed for the frontier.

Publications

Background to the Plantation

- *The Scottish Migration to Ulster in the Reign of James I* by M. Perceval-Maxwell (Ulster Historical Foundation, Belfast, 1990)

This book describes in detail the initial establishment of Scottish settlement in the province of Ulster in the period 1603 to 1625. In addition, the book includes short biographies of the principal planters; namely of nine "Chief Scottish Undertakers," fifty "Ordinary Scottish Undertakers," and two "Scottish Servitors." These men acquired estates in Ulster of 1,000 acres or more.

- *The Plantation of Ulster* by Philip Robinson
  (Ulster Historical Foundation, Belfast, 1994)

This account of the Plantation of Ulster discusses the emergence of settlement patterns where "Scots Dissenters, English Protestants and native Irish Catholics each consolidated their own territories.' In addition, this book tabulates, by county and barony, the estates – by name of grantee – granted to "Servitors," "Major Irish grantees," "English undertakers," "Scottish undertakers," "London companies," "Corporate towns," and "School lands.'"

- *The Cromwellian Settlement of Ireland* by John P Prendergast (1865)

This book is the recognized source on the Cromwellian settlement of Ireland in the 1650s. In the period known as the Commonwealth from 1649 to 1660, England was ruled by a Puritan-dominated Parliament. With the English Civil War over, Oliver Cromwell turned his attention to Ireland, where in 1641 the native Irish had risen in revolt. Cromwell and his army of 12,000 men crushed the rebellion within one year.

On 26 September 1653 the English Parliament passed an Act for the new planting of Ireland with English colonists. The adventurers who had funded Cromwell's army in Ireland and the officers and soldiers who had served in it were to receive land (as their payment) in the provinces of Leinster, Munster and Ulster.

Eleven million acres of land was confiscated. The province of Connacht was reserved for the "habitation of the Irish Nation," where they were to transplant their wives and children before 1st May 1654, under the penalty of death.

Pedigrees of Plantation Families

- *Burke's Peerage & Baronetage* (1860)
- *Burke's Landed Gentry of Ireland* (1958)
- *Burke's Irish Family Records* (1976)

The criteria for inclusion of a detailed family history in Burke's publications can be summarized as follows:

1. Hereditary Peerage. Family histories of hereditary titled families (i.e. from Dukes to Baronets) published in *Burke's Peerage and Baronetage*.
2. By 1900 the criterion for inclusion was territorial. Pedigrees of the Landed Gentry (with no titles) were now published. In England, the family histories of distinguished, untitled, County families were published. In Ireland Landed Gentry equated to ownership of about 1,000 acres of land. With Land Acts from 1903 the big estates were broken up. However, the 1958 edition of Burke's was still called *The Landed Gentry of Ireland*. This book included the family histories of merchants and industrialists, who, as a mark of their success, tended to live in grand country houses.
3. With the 1976 edition the pedigrees of non-landed families were extensively recorded. Burke's was now seen as a "book of dynasties." Criterion for inclusion in *Burke's Irish Family Records* (1976) was stated as: "families should have been distinguished in one period in Ireland for more than one generation" in the church, politics, the arts, sciences, professions or through ownership of land and houses.

Biographies of Planters

- The *Dictionary of Irish Biography*

The Dictionary of Irish Biography is Ireland's national biographical dictionary. Devised, researched, written and edited under the auspices of the Royal Irish Academy, its online edition covers nearly 11,000 lives. Further details can be found at **www.ria.ie/research-projects/dictionary-irish-biography**.

- *History of the Irish Parliament 1692-1800* by Edith Mary Johnston-Liik
  (Ulster Historical Foundation, Belfast, 2002)

This book includes detailed biographies of 2,300 Members of Parliament (MP), usually members of "Landed Gentry," who represented Irish constituencies in the Irish Parliament between 1692-1800.

- *Fighters of Derry Their Deeds and Descendants: Being a Chronicle of Events in Ireland during the Revolutionary Period 1688-1691* by William R Young (1932)

This book is a unique and unrivalled source for tracing 17th-century Plantation ancestors. This book names and, in many cases, provides biographical detail of 1,660 "Defenders" and 352 officers of the "Jacobite Army." The term "Defenders" in Young's book refers to much more than just simply a list of those who were documented as playing their part in the defense of Londonderry during the famous Siege of Derry of 1689; it refers to all those people who were named in contemporary sources and accounts as playing an active or supportive role in the successful Williamite campaign of 1689 to 1691.

It is very evident in any examination of Young's book that many of the Defenders are first-, second-, third- or fourth-generation descendants of Scottish, English and Welsh planters. In many cases Young connects the Defenders of 1689-1691 to the original planters who settled in Ireland.

- *Three Hundred Years in Inishowen* by Amy Isabel Young (1929)

This book provides detailed family histories and charts of many Plantation families of Derry, and Inishowen, County Donegal

- *A History of Congregations in the Presbyterian Church in Ireland 1610-1982*
  (Presbyterian Historical Society of Ireland, Belfast, 1982)

This book provides a brief history, in alphabetical order by name of congregation, of all Presbyterian congregations in Ireland together with brief biographies of Presbyterian ministers in Irish congregations between 1610 and 1982.

Record Sources

Church Registers

Church registers of baptisms, marriages and burials, with their ability to build and confirm family links, are the building blocks of family history. Church registers should always be examined once you know the parish location of your ancestor. Public Record Office of Northern Ireland's *Guide to Church Records*, which can be accessed on their website at **www.nidirect.gov.uk/publications/proni-guide-church-records** lists, in alphabetical order by civil parish, church registers of all denominations for most parishes in Ulster and their commencement dates. Microfilm copies of the majority of these church registers can be examined in the Public Record Office of Northern Ireland (PRONI).

Researching Scots-Irish Ancestors: The essential genealogical guide to early modern Ulster, 1600-1800, by William J Roulston (Ulster Historical Foundation, Belfast, 2018), is a comprehensive and unrivalled guide to record sources for this period. It includes a full listing, in alphabetical order by civil parish, of all pre-1800 church records for Ulster.

It must be said, however, that it is quite possible that researchers will not be able to confirm the birth, marriage and burial details of their ancestor, as only a relatively small percentage of church registers in Ulster predate 1800. Unfortunately, it is a very common problem in Ireland that churches, of all denominations, are much older than their surviving registers.

Census Substitutes

With a few notable exceptions, church registers are frequently irrelevant, owing to their non-existence, to family historians seeking 17th- and 18th-century ancestors in Ulster. The most realistic, and simplest, strategy is to examine surviving census substitutes, often compiled by civil parish, for any references to a surname of interest. The most important of these are:

- Muster Rolls of 1630 (when landlords mustered their tenants to identify adult males capable of military service)
- Hearth Money Rolls of the 1660s (a tax raised for every hearth or fireplace)
- Protestant Householders' Lists of 1740
- Religious Census of 1766
- Flax Growers' Lists of 1796

Transcripts and copies of many of these sources can be found in the Public Record Office of Northern Ireland (PRONI). You can search a number of 18th-century census substitutes for Northern Ireland, such as indexes to pre-1858 wills, 1740 Protestant Householders' Lists, Religious Census of 1766, and 1775 Dissenters' Petitions in PRONI'S "Name Search" archive at **www.nidirect.gov.uk/information-and-services/search-archives-online/name-search**.

At "The Scots in Ulster" website, **www.ancestryireland.com/scotsinulster**, you can search, by surname, early-17th-century Muster Rolls, Hearth Money Rolls of the 1660s, Protestant Householders' Lists of 1740 and the Flax Growers' Lists of 1796.

From a family historian's point of view, it is disappointing that these census substitutes name heads of household only. Because no information is provided on family members within each household or relationships between householders, it is not possible to confirm the nature of linkages between named people in these sources. Census substitutes, however, are very useful in confirming the presence of a family name in a particular townland and/or parish.

Estate Records

In the 17th and 18th centuries, the majority of the population of Ireland lived on large estates, until they were finally broken up in the latter years of the 19th century under the Land Acts. The administration of these estates by landlords and their agents produced a large quantity of records, including maps, rentals, account books, leases, title deeds and surveys.

If you know the townland your ancestor lived in or farmed, and the name of their landlord, then you should consider an examination of any relevant estate records. The Public Record Office of Northern Ireland (PRONI) holds the largest collection of estate records in Northern Ireland, which are detailed, by county, in their *Guide to Landed Estate Records*. You can also search their eCatalogue online for relevant estate papers at **www.nidirect.gov.uk/services/search-pronis-ecatalogue**.

William Roulston's *Researching Scots-Irish Ancestors: The essential genealogical guide to early modern Ulster, 1600-1800* also provides detailed descriptions of 250 estate collections, in alphabetical order by estate (usually surname of the landlord), for each of the nine counties of Ulster.

Corporation Records

In the 17th and 18th centuries, local government in towns was controlled by a corporation. Most corporations, i.e. corporate towns, in Ulster were 17th-century creations, mostly of the years 1610-1613. Indeed, in the initial plan of Plantation 26 corporate towns were proposed: 4 in County Armagh, 3 in Cavan, 7 in Donegal, 3 in Fermanagh, 5 in Tyrone and 4 in Coleraine (renamed Londonderry in 1613).

Records relating to 18 corporations have survived and include minute books and lists of freemen. William Roulston's *Researching Scots-Irish Ancestors: The essential genealogical guide to early modern Ulster, 1600-1800* lists surviving corporation records under the relevant parish in Appendix 1, which provides a summary listing of genealogical sources for every civil parish in the nine counties of Ulster for the period 1600-1800.

For example, the Minute Books of Londonderry Corporation, from 1673-1901, can be browsed online at the website **www.nidirect.gov.uk/information-and-services/search-archives-online/londonderry-corporation-records**.

Sir William Petty's census of 1659 names 47 persons of standing, consisting of 23 classified as Gentry and a further 24 as merchants, residing within the walled city of Londonderry. It was from this select group and their descendants that the Common Council of Londonderry Corporation was formed.

Hence, the minute books of Londonderry Corporation will be a good starting pointing for any researcher wishing to explore the landed gentry and merchant community of 17th- and 18th-century Derry. Each set of minutes begins with date of the meeting of the Common Council and list of members in attendance. According to the Charter of 1613, the city was to have a mayor, two sheriffs, a chamberlain, 12 aldermen and 24 burgesses who were to form the common council or Corporation.

In a city dominated by merchants, shopkeepers and craftsmen, only freemen of the city were entitled to conduct business, own property and receive protection within the walled city. To be able to trade within the City Walls or liberties of Londonderry you had to be registered as a freeman. Hence, the minute books detail the petitions of those seeking freedom of the city.

Registry of Deeds

The Registry of Deeds, located in Henrietta Street, Dublin, holds a variety of records relating to property transactions, such as leases, wills, marriage settlements and other deeds, dating back to 1708. While the original purpose of the Registry of Deeds was to enforce rules limiting the land transactions of Catholics, even before the removal of these rules in 1782 many Catholics and representatives of Catholic families appear in the memorials. Many memorials, i.e. sworn copies of deeds, were registered by merchants and traders, as well as landed gentry, to provide some form of security of tenure.

It is now feasible to search this complex source, owing to the transcription work of "Registry of Deeds Index Project Ireland" at **http://irishdeedsindex.net/search/index.php**.

1641 Rebellion

In 1641 the Plantation of Ulster faced its first serious crisis. On 22 October 1641 the native Irish, under Sir Phelim O'Neill, rose in rebellion in Counties Derry and Tyrone, and the walled city of Londonderry became a refuge for Protestant settlers. By April 1642 the city was close to starvation, with the rebel forces led by Sir Phelim O'Neill camped at Strabane. However, the threatened siege of Derry was lifted on 17 May 1642 by the defeat of the Irish army, led by the O'Cahans (O'Kanes), near Dungiven, County Derry by an army consisting of east Donegal settlers and four companies of soldiers from Derry city.

The 1641 Depositions at Trinity College Dublin Library consist of transcripts and images of all 8,000 depositions, examinations and associated materials in which Protestant men and women of all classes told of their experiences following the outbreak of the rebellion by the Catholic Irish in October 1641. A fully searchable digital edition of the 1641 Depositions can be examined at **http://1641.tcd.ie**.

The Down Survey of Ireland, 1656-58

The Down Survey of 1656-1658 maps out in great detail the dramatic transfer in land ownership from Catholics to Protestants in 17th-century Ireland. These maps can be examined at **http://downsurvey.tcd.ie/down-survey-maps.php**.

CASE STUDY: TRACING THE SCOTS-IRISH ANCESTRY OF ABRAHAM HILLHOUSE

In this case study, a variety of sources are used in researching the 17th- and 18th-century family history of the Scots-Irish Hillhouse family of County Derry.

It would appear that the younger, ambitious sons of English landed gentry and Scottish lairds, who were not going to inherit the family manor, took prominent roles in the various military campaigns and plantations of Ireland, and of North America, in the 17th century.

Starting Point

Family tradition in the United States records that Samuel Hillhouse, born c.1707, was from Limavady, County Derry and came to America as a young man. His parents were John and Rachel and they had a house/estate called Free Hall or Freehall, and his grandfather Abraham came from Failford, Ayrshire, Scotland.

Identifying the Location of Freehall

The key to unlocking Scots-Irish family history origins is the knowledge of place. An examination of the *Townland Index* reveals three townlands called Freehall in County Derry. Of particular interest, based on the above family tradition, is the townland of "Free Hall or Moneyvennon" in the civil parish of Aghanloo, as it is located three miles northeast of the town of Limavady.

At the 17th-century Plantation of Ulster, with settlers from England and Scotland, Freehall or Moneyvennon in Aghanloo parish was granted to the Haberdashers' Company of the city of London (**www.haberdashers.co.uk**).

Most of the Haberdashers' proportion was located in Aghanloo parish. The castle and bawn of the Habersdashers stood on the River Roe at a place known as Ballycastle, which was probably the site of a Norman castle. The Haberdashers built a linear village at Artikelly, one mile from their castle, consisting of one street with two rows of thatched single-story cottages set in rectangular plots. Freehall was located one mile to the east of the castle at Ballycastle and one mile to the northeast of the village of Artikelly.

Church Registers

Church registers of baptisms, marriages and burials, with their ability to build and confirm family links, are the building blocks of family history. Church registers should always be examined once you know the parish location of your ancestor.

It must be said, however, that it is quite possible researchers will not be able to confirm the birth, marriage and death details of their ancestor, as only a relatively small percentage of church registers in Ulster predate 1800. Unfortunately, it is a very common problem in Ireland that churches, of all denominations, are much older than their surviving registers.

With a few notable exceptions, church registers are frequently irrelevant, owing to their nonexistence, to family historians seeking 17th- and 18th-century ancestors in Ulster.

Unfortunately, there are no surviving 17th- or 18th-century church registers for Aghanloo parish. Some 18th-century content, from 1728, with significant gaps, survives for the nearby town of Limavady in the registers of Drumachose Parish Church, but no references to Hillhouse were identified.

It is always worth checking the registers of the Church of Ireland (Protestant) Cathedral as it was in effect the Parish Church of the Diocese; in the case of the Diocese of Derry, that is St. Columb's Cathedral (**www.stcolumbscathedral.org**) in Derry city, 16 miles west of Limavady, whose registers date back to 1642. An examination of its registers of baptisms, marriages and burials (which have been transcribed, indexed and published in three books from 1642 to 1775) reveal seven Hillhouse burial entries (including potential spelling variations of the surname):

> Died: 17 November 1700, Mary, daughter of James and Lettis Hillis
> Died: 28 August 1702, Henry, son of William and Lettis Hillis
> Died: 6 November 1705, Jane, daughter of William and Lettis Hilhous
> Died: 4 September 1714, Ann wife of William Hillows
> Died: 12 June 1730, Ann, wife of Abraham Hillhouse
> Died: 2 June 1730, Forgison, son of Abraham and Ann Hillhouse
> Died: 27 May 1732, John Hillhouse

Beyond Church Registers

A basic problem facing those tracing the family origins of 17th- and 18th-century Irish ancestors is that once your research extends beyond church registers (which are the building blocks of Irish family history) you have few means, unless the family history has been documented and passed down through the generations, to confirm family connections. Quite simply, the birth, marriage and death details of many of our 17th- and 18th-century ancestors have not survived in a written record source.

Quite often the only realistic strategy in tracing ancestors beyond church registers of baptisms, marriages and burials is to examine surviving land records and census substitutes, often compiled by civil parish, for any references to a surname or given name of interest.

The basic problem with these sources is that they name heads of household only; hence they provide insufficient information to confirm the nature of linkages between named people in these sources. Census substitutes, however, are very useful in confirming the presence of a family name in a particular townland and/or parish, and in providing some insight into the frequency and distribution of surnames.

However, I aim to demonstrate that a wide range of sources are available and that an examination of them confirms that the Hillhouse family was a significant family in the Limavady area throughout the 17th and 18th centuries. Indeed an examination of these sources reveals that two Hillhouse families were settled in County Derry from the early years of the Plantation of Ulster, i.e. prior to the1641 Rebellion, one in Freehall, Limavady and the other in Dunboe parish, Coleraine.

Wills

An examination of the *Indexes to Irish Wills: Volume V, Derry and Raphoe, 1612-1858* (edited by Gertrude Thrift, Phillimore & Co, London, 1920) identified the following 17th-century Hillhouse entries in County Derry:

Name and Residence	Date of Probate
Hillhous, Abraham, Ardikelly, parish Aghanloo	1676
Hillhous, Adam, Dunboe	1635

Hence, it would appear that Abraham Hillhouse died c. 1676 at Ardikelly (spelled as Artikelly today) in the parish of Aghanloo and that an Adam Hillhouse died c. 1635 in Dunboe parish (just to the west of the town of Coleraine). Of course, what this source can't do is tell us the nature of the link, if any, between Abraham of Artikelly and Adam of Dunboe.

The Great Parchment Book

Abraham Hillhouse was settled in Limavady by 1639 as his name is recorded in "The Great Parchment Book." Held in London Metropolitan Archives, the Great Parchment Book was damaged by fire in London's Guildhall in 1786 and it was conserved and digitized, in 2013, at **www.greatparchmentbook.org**, as the City of London's contribution to commemorations in Derry of the 400th anniversary of the building of the city walls.

The Great Parchment Book of The Honourable The Irish Society was a major survey carried out by a Commission from King Charles I under the Great Seal dated 11 March 1639 of all those estates in County Londonderry managed by the City of London through the Irish Society and the City of London livery companies. Charles I claimed the estates (constituting the entire county of Londonderry) as forfeit, ruling that the Londoners had not fulfilled their obligations of plantation. The Commission's purpose was to seize on the King's behalf all castles, manors, lands and tenements lately belonging to the Londoners and to conclude new contracts for leases with existing tenants and others.

The Great Parchment Book returns one folio concerning Abraham Hilhouse (gentleman) in Haberdashers' Proportion, which reads:

"On 17 August 1639, the Commissioners concluded and agreed that Robert McLeland, Gavin Kelsoe, Hugh Boyle, Alexander [?], Abraham Hilhouse and John McLeland shall have and hold all those six townlands called Artikelly, [?], Gortamoney, Maheraskeagh, Tullaherrenmore and Tullaherrenbegg in Aghanloo and have one weekly market on Wednesday in the town of Artikelly and three yearly fairs in town of Artikelly."

Hearth Money Roll of 1663

The Hillhouse family were clearly a significant family in Limavady throughout the 17th and 18th centuries, as their name is recorded in many sources.

Abraham Hilhouse of Aghanloo parish (townland not specified) was enumerated for taxation purposes in the Hearth Money Roll of 1663.

The Minute Books of Borough of Limavady

By 1665 Abraham Hillhouse was a serving Burgess of Limavady Corporation and in that same year John Hillhouse and William Hillhouse were "admitted and sworn Freemen" of Limavady.

Sir Thomas Phillips described as "a pushing soldier of fortune" first arrived in Ireland as a military commander in 1599, and in 1610 he was granted 13,100 acres of land at Limavady, which included O'Cahan's castle, on a cliff overhanging the River Roe. One mile from the castle he commenced the building of the "Newtown of Limavady," which was laid out in a cruciform road pattern. By 1622, 18 one-story houses and an inn had been built and they were centered on the crossroads that contained a flagpole, a cross and stocks.

Newtown-Limavady (known as Limavady from 1870) was incorporated as a town on 31 March 1613 with a charter granted by King James I. According to this charter the town was to appoint a Provost and 12 Burgesses who were to form the common council or Corporation, and to return 2 Members of Parliament (which ceased with the Act of Union that created, in 1801, the United Kingdom of Great Britain and Ireland).

It was from a select group of landed gentry and merchants and their descendants that the Common Council of Limavady Corporation was formed. Hence, the minute books of Limavady Corporation are a good starting pointing for any researcher wishing to explore the landed gentry and merchant community of 17th- and 18th-century Limavady. To conduct trade in the Borough you had to be registered as a freeman; hence the minute books detail the petitions of those seeking to become freemen.

Corporation Records, i.e. the minute books of the Common Council of Limavady Corporation, date from 1659. Each set of minutes begins with date of the meeting of the Common Council and list of members in attendance. Edited abstracts from these minute books have been transcribed and published in *Records of the Town of Limavady, 1609 to 1808 by* E. M. F-G Boyle (published 1912, republished as *Boyle's Records of Limavady, 1609 to 1808* by North-West Books, Limavady, 1989). The following Hillhouse references are recorded:

Corporation Meeting of 24 June 1665
In attendance, Abraham Hillhouse, Burgess of the Corporation of Newtown-Limavady.
John Hillhouse and William Hillhouse were 'admitted and sworn Freemen'.

Corporation Meeting of 24 June 1696
William Hillhouse sworn Freeman.

Corporation Meeting of 29 September 1708
William Hillhouse sworn Freeman.

Corporation Meeting of 14 October 1718
In attendance, William Hillhouse, Constable.

The Registry of Deeds

An examination of the records of the Registry of Deeds confirm that the Hillhouse family was still residing at Freehall, near Limavady, in the middle years of the 18th century. In 1745 the estate of Freehall passed from Abraham Hillhouse to his son Abraham James Hillhouse, who was a merchant in London, and in 1757 Abraham Hillhouse of Freehall married Ann Ferguson, daughter of Reverend Andrew Ferguson of Burt, County Donegal.

The Registry of Deeds, located in Henrietta Street, Dublin, holds a variety of records relating to property transactions, such as leases, wills, marriage settlements and other deeds, dating back to 1708. Many memorials, i.e. sworn copies of deeds, were registered by merchants and traders, as well as landed gentry, to provide some form of security of tenure.

An examination of the "Registry of Deeds Index Project Ireland," searchable at **http://irishdeedsindex.net/search/index.php**, returned nine search results for surname Hillhouse. These included:

Memorial Number 82070: Deed of Assignment of 'Estate of Freehall, and the Maine in co Londonderry' from Abraham Hillhouse senior, Gentleman to his son Abraham James Hillhouse junior, dated 16 September 1745.

Memorial Number 119,409: Abraham James Hillhouse, merchant of London, on 16 December 1758, leased and released 'Freehall & the Main, co Londonderry' to David Latouche of city of Dublin.

Memorial Number 123,629: Marriage settlement, dated 17 February 1757 of Abraham Hillhouse, Gentleman of Freehall, co Londonderry to Ann Ferguson, daughter of Rev Andrew Ferguson, of Burt, co Donegal of 'dowery out of Moneyvennon commonly known by Freehall and Upper & Lower Main, & live in the mansion house of Freehall in her widowhood.'

1641 Rebellion

In 1641 the Plantation of Ulster faced its first serious crisis. On 22 October 1641 the native Irish, under Sir Phelim O'Neill, rose in rebellion in Counties Derry and Tyrone, and the walled city of Londonderry became a refuge for Protestant settlers. A "League of the Captains of Londonderry" was set up to guard the city, with the raising of nine companies of foot soldiers, each assigned with a particular section of the walls of Derry to repair and to defend. By April 1642 the city was close to starvation, with the rebel forces led by Sir Phelim O'Neill camped at Strabane. However, the threatened siege of Derry was lifted on 17 May 1642 by the defeat of the Irish army, led by the O'Cahans (O'Kanes), near Dungiven, County Derry by an army consisting of east Donegal settlers and four Companies of soldiers from Derry city.

A fully searchable digital edition of the 1641 Depositions at Trinity College Dublin Library can be searched at **http://1641.tcd.ie**. The 1641 Depositions consist of transcripts and images of all 8,000 depositions, examinations and associated materials in which Protestant men and women of all classes told of their experiences following the outbreak of the rebellion by the Catholic Irish in October 1641.

A surname search of "Hilhouse" records four depositions relating to the death of John Hilhouse of Gortycavan in Dunboe Parish, County Derry, three miles west of the town of Coleraine.

Seemingly, after defeating and killing a party of English and Scottish men garrisoned at Garvagh, County Derry about 20 December 1641, Rory Duffe McCormacke and his brothers Art and Edmund McCormacke and about 30-40 men armed with long pikes set upon the British at "Gortecavan in the parish of Dunboe" and killed John Hilhouse.

It is possible, but not proven, that John Hilhouse of Gortycavan, Dunboe parish, who died during the 1641 Rebellion, was the son of Adam Hilhous of Dunboe whose will was proved in 1635.

Fighters of Derry

Nearly 50 years later the Plantation of Ulster faced another potential reversal to its fortunes in the events surrounding the 1689 Siege of Derry, and a Captain Abraham Hillhouse of Coleraine is recorded as a "defender" of Derry.

William R. Young's *Fighters of Derry Their Deeds and Descendants: Being a Chronicle of Events in Ireland during the Revolutionary Period 1688-1691* (published by Eyre and Spottiswoode, London, 1932) is a unique and unrivalled source for tracing 17th-century Plantation of Ulster ancestors. This book names and, in many cases, provides biographical detail of 1,660 "Defenders" and 352 officers of the "Jacobite Army."

The term "Defenders" in Young's book refers to much more than just simply a list of those who were documented as playing their part in the defense of Londonderry during the famous Siege of Derry, which commenced with the closing of its gates on 7 December 1688 and ended on 31 July 1689 with the Jacobite army in retreat after a relief fleet, with essential food supplies, managed to break through the boom of fir and iron cable across the River Foyle.

'Defenders' refers to all those people who were named in contemporary sources and accounts as playing an active or supportive role in the successful Williamite campaign of 1689 to 1691.

The Williamite War in Ireland, 1689-1691, was, in effect, the struggle for the English throne between the deposed James II, the last Catholic monarch of the three Kingdoms of England, Scotland and Ireland who had the support of Louis XIV of France, and William of Orange with the backing of the English Parliament.

The successful Williamite campaign included the defense of Derry during the Siege of 18 April to 31 July 1689; the harrying of Jacobite forces in Connacht and Ulster by locally raised regiments operating out of Enniskillen throughout 1689; victories at the Battle of the Boyne on 1 July 1690 and the Battle of Aughrim (County Galway) on 12 July 1691; and the final Irish surrender of Limerick on 23 September 1691.

As well as naming Defenders of Derry, Young's book names those who were involved in the Enniskillen campaigns and in other battles such as the Boyne. It also names the prominent supporters of Protestant interests throughout Ireland at this time, including those named on the list of attainted in James' Dublin parliament. James II's Parliament, which met in Dublin on 7 May 1689 and sat for three weeks, passed "The Bill of Attainder," which confiscated estates and condemned without trial over 2,500 persons, of whom 921 were from Ulster, of high treason. This book lists:

Defender 739: 'Captain Abraham Hillhouse, of Coleraine, defender, so described, is among the attainted in James' Dublin Parliament, and his signature is on the address to King William after the relief' [i.e. after the lifting of the Siege of Derry of 1689].

Condemnation of Assassination Attempt on William III in 1696

In the Corporation of Londonderry Minute Book of 16 April 1696 (pp132-133, Volume 2, January 1688 to 20 July 1704) are, tabulated in three columns, the names of 226 citizens of the city of Londonderry who signed a resolution expressing condemnation of the plot to assassinate King William. A James Hillhouse was recorded as one of these signatories.

William III ruled jointly, from 1689, with his wife, Mary II, until her death on 28 December 1694. There was a considerable surge in support for William, who reigned as King of England, Scotland and Ireland until his death on 8 March 1702, following the exposure of a Jacobite plan to assassinate him in 1696.

Corporation of Londonderry Minute Books, which date from 1673, can be browsed online at **www.nidirect.gov.uk/information-and-services/search-archives-online/londonderry-corporation-records.**

Local History Publications

Local History publications can provide a wealth of material on history of families and of place. Charles Knowles Bolton in *Scotch Irish Pioneers in Ulster and America* (first published in 1910), on page 113, writes:

"The Rev. James Hillhouse was born about 1688, the son of John and Rachel Hillhouse, owners of a large estate called Freehall, in County Londonderry. He studied at Glasgow under the famous Professor Simson, and was ordained by Derry presbytery October 15, 1718. Coming to America in 1720, he was called to a church in the second parish of New London in 1722, where he died December 15, 1740. His son William was a member of the Continental Congress, and William's son James was a Senator of the United States."

With all this information the following family tree linking the Hillhouse family in Scotland, Ireland and America can be constructed:

```
                Abraham Hillhouse
                b. Failford, Ayrshire, Scotland
                settled at Freehall, Aghanloo parish, County Londonderry
                d. 1676
                    |
                John Hillhouse           =        Rachel
                Owner of Freehall estate,         |
                County Londonderry                |
                                Rev. James Hillhouse
                                b. 1688
                                emigrated to America in 1720
                                d. 15 December 1740
                                    |
                                William Hillhouse
                                Member of Continental Congress
                                    |
                                James Hillhouse
                                Senator of the United States
```